METROPOLITAN HOUSING MARKET

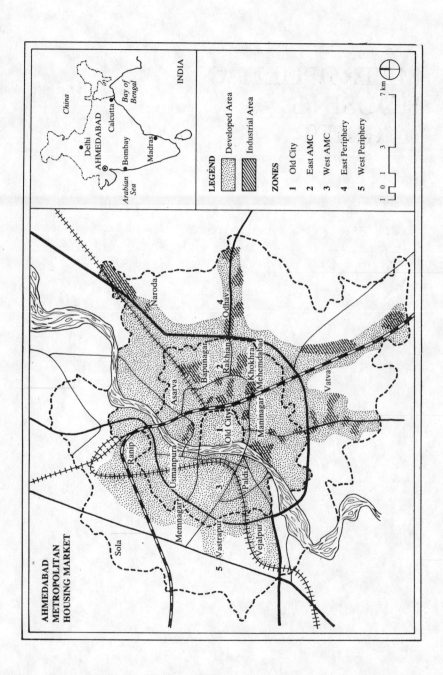

METROPOLITAN HOUSING MARKET

A Study of Ahmedabad

MEERA MEHTA
And
DINESH MEHTA

Assisted by
H.M. SHIVANAND SWAMY

SAGE PUBLICATIONS
New Delhi/Newbury Park/London

First published in 1989 by

Sage Publications India Pvt. Ltd.
M-32 Greater Kailash Market-I
New Delhi 110 048

Sage Publications Inc 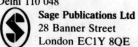 **Sage Publications Ltd**
2111 West Hillcrest Drive 28 Banner Street
Newbury Park, California 91320 London EC1Y 8QE

Published by Tejeshwar Singh for Sage Publications India Pvt Ltd, phototypeset by Aurelec Data Processing Systems, Pondicherry, and printed at Chaman Offset Printers, Delhi.

Library of Congress Cataloging-in-Publication Data
Mehta, Meera, 1949–
    Metropolitan housing market: a study of Ahmedabad / Meera Mehta and Dinesh Mehta, assisted by H.M. Shivanand Swamy.
    p.cm
    Bibliography: p.
    1. Housing—India—Ahmedābād. I. Mehta, Dinesh. II. Shivanand Swamy, H.M. III. Title.
    HD7361.A53M43   1989   363.5'0954'75—dc 20   89–35559

ISBN: 0-8039-9596-2 (U.S.A.)
    81-7036-142-7 (India)

Contents

List of Tables

Abbreviations

AMC	Ahmedabad Municipal Corporation
AUDA	Ahmedabad Urban Development Authority
AUA	Ahmedabad Urban Agglomeration
CBRI	Central Building Research Institute
DDA	Delhi Development Authority
EIS	Environmental Improvement Scheme
EMI	Employment Market Information
EWS	Economically Weaker Section
GCHFC	Gujarat Cooperative Housing Finance Corporation
GHB	Gujarat Housing Board
GSCB	Gujarat Slum Clearance Board
HDFC	Housing Development Finance Corporation
HIG	High Income Group
HUDCO	Housing and Urban Development Corporation
LIG	Low Income Group
MIG	Middle Income Group
NBO	National Building Organisation
NSS	National Sample Survey
SIHS	Subsidised Industrial Housing Scheme
ULC (ULCRA)	Urban Land (Ceiling and Regulations) Act

Preface

The School of Planning, Ahmedabad, is primarily an academic institution, imparting education in urban and regional planning. Since its inception, the basic philosophy of planning education at the School has differed from the mainstream urban planning approach of physical land-use plan preparation, to focus explicitly on the socio-economic aspects of urban development.

In this perspective, the present research is our modest attempt to initiate the process of understanding local housing market behaviour—a research area so far largely ignored by urban scholars in India. The research framework can be replicated to generate similar studies in other metropolitan areas and secondary cities. It is our firm belief that such research findings will not only help in the identification of housing strategies and programmes at the local level but would also provide significant guidelines for national and state level policies.

It is coincidental that this study, initiated in December 1984, was delayed due to prolonged civil disturbances in Ahmedabad during 1985 and has reached its present shape in the International Year of Shelter for the Homeless (IYSH). Though our study bears no direct relationship to the activities under IYSH, we hope it provides a critical input to the associated processes at work in the country, such as, the formulation of the Draft National Housing Policy, the work of the National Commission on Urbanisation and the upcoming National Campaign of Housing Rights.

Amongst the many individuals with whom we had initial discussions regarding the nature of this study, we would like to express our sincere gratitude to Dr. Rakesh Mohan who motivated us and suggested possibilities of financial assistance. He painstakingly went through our initial draft proposal and together we had many fruitful discussions. Even while away in Washington, he ensured a steady stream of relevant research documents from which we greatly benefited. His comments on the research report have been extremely valuable.

Dr. Y.K. Alagh, whose teachings initiated both of us into economic planning, provided the necessary encouragement and help in ensuring the required research funds from the Planning Commission. We are grateful to him and the members of the Research Committee of the Planning Commission for providing financial support.

Many researchers (and friends) have honoured us by spending time in reading the research report and offering extremely positive and constructive comments and suggestions. We would especially like to thank Dr. D.B. Gupta, Paul Baross, Kiran Wadhwa and Peter Nientied for their comments and encouragement. Pariseema Trivedi, a student at the School, and Shrenik Shah, a practising architect in the city, helped us untangle the web of processes involved in private sector housing supply. Discussions with private estate developers also strengthened our understanding. Officials in the City Corporation, particularly Shri N.R. Desai, and in the public housing agencies readily parted with information. We are thankful to all of them for their cooperation. The staff at the Physical Research Laboratory's Computer Centre provided the initial help in data processing. Subsequently, the entire data analysis was carried out at the recently installed computer system at our own Institute. Utpal Sharma has prepared the map.

At the School, Mr. B.V. Doshi, founder-member of CEPT, has always motivated us to go beyond our routine academic activities towards research and professional pursuits. Dr. R.N. Vakil, Honorary Dean of CEPT, and the administrative staff have provided the necessary support. Haripriya Rangan and Anand Tatu also worked with us for some time on this project. Devanand, who has been with us as a secretary-typist for this project, worked diligently to meet the self-imposed deadlines of the project. Besides the excellent typing support, he also provided occasional research assistance.

Shivanand Swamy, who began with us as the principal research associate for this project, continued with us till its completion despite getting other lucrative offers during the course of the project. His total involvement and consistent help right through the project has been instrumental in our completing it.

This study was sponsored by the Planning Commission, New Delhi, and was financed by a grant from it. The Planning Commission, however, accepts no responsibility for the facts, opinions and interpretations expressed in the book. It, of course, goes without saying that we are responsible for any errors which still remain.

For a wife and husband team of researchers, such projects entail a heavy demand on domestic chores as well. Urmee and Dheer, our children, have well withstood the lack of attention to them with deep understanding and put up admirably with our endless discussions.

Ahmedabad
December 1988

Meera Mehta
Dinesh Mehta

1. Introduction

In the political rhetoric of Third World governments, housing is regarded as one of the basic needs. Despite this recognition, in terms of public policies and investments, housing has generally received a very low priority. Meagre resources have failed to make any significant impact on the housing situation of a large segment of the population. Whether one looks at the situation in aggregate terms at the national level or at the city level, the evidence overwhelmingly points to a deterioration of the housing situation. especially for households in the lower income strata. Even for the few indicators which show some improvement, the benefits have accrued disproportionately to the better-off sections of society.

It is, however, heartening to note that over the last four decades housing policies have undergone some changes in India. To begin with, there is a very explicit acceptance at the policy level of support policies which rely on indirect measures to influence the pattern of supply. In accordance with this, there have been attempts to evolve strategies related especially to land and finance, and a change in the usual approach of packaged product to a progressive development model. The scanty available evaluation of these measures, however, does not present a very encouraging picture. There have been some attempts to understand this lack of success within a political economy perspective which emphasises the interrelationship between individual actions, social processes and public policy.

A second aspect of change in the approach to planning is an awareness of the need to evolve housing policy perspectives at the state level and, especially, housing strategies at the local urban area level. This is partly also related to an understanding of the fact that the newer progressive development approaches are not likely to work unless they are firmly linked to an overall urban housing strategy. Local governments today do not maintain an adequate information base to assess the housing condition of their residents. If these agencies are expected to play a positive role in generating a climate which is conducive even for the private sector to cater to the housing needs of the urban poor, then, in addition to the basic information, these agencies must also understand the local market in terms of the supply processes and the residential choice behaviour.

In broad terms the housing problem can be described as follows: a mismatch between housing supply and demand which leads to a lack of adequate and decent housing at affordable prices, with required amenities and with secured tenure, at accessible locations, in safe and congenial environments, with adequate services and facilities. Housing is not a mere provision of shelter, but is a far more complex problem involving all the above issues.

Conventional analyses of the housing problem in India have, however, been limited to estimating housing needs, shortages and the corresponding financial requirements. In the wake of the government's gradual shift towards housing support policies, it becomes imperative that the nature of housing analysis should also move away from examining just the magnitude of dwelling units required, towards a more comprehensive analysis of the processes of housing supply and demand. Such systemic studies will not only aid the evolution of rational housing policies at the central and local levels but also help in the formulation of housing programmes and project design. Part of the efforts within these housing support policies will undoubtedly be in the urban areas of the country, where the housing problem has reached alarming proportions. Given the fact that the urban population of India is estimated to double by the turn of this century, it is necessary to evolve meaningful housing policies which would both alleviate the existing housing situation and effectively deal with the problems that will result from the increased population in urban areas.

This study of the Ahmedabad housing market was carried out within the framework of the above perspective. The study seeks to provide insights into various aspects related to the processes of supply and demand in the Ahmedabad urban area, and to discuss their implications for policy guidelines.

Our examination of earlier research revealed that the bulk of the existing literature, especially for developing countries, is restricted to examining the housing demand. There are very few attempts to look at the supply side and still fewer which examine both supply and demand aspects in an equilibrium framework. Our approach in this study is to separately examine the supply process and the residential choice behaviour. The only integration of the two is in terms of their influences on each other. The housing market is segmented and hence the supply process relating to different segments and the residential behaviour of various classes of consumers are of particular interest to us. On the supply side, our emphasis has been on the changing supply processes and their impact on different sections of the population. This has been done by tracing the significance and growth trends of different housing sub-markets using the criteria of location, house type and developer type over a period of time. These estimations have generally been done by collating a large number of secondary sources and combining them with detailed discussions with various actors in the supply process.

The residential choice behaviour is analysed in terms of housing demand and willingness to pay, housing preferences and priorities, and the constraints which inhibit utility maximisation. This analysis is based mainly on a cross-sectional analysis of the housing situation, expenditure and satisfaction. However, some attempt is also made to look at housing careers, in terms of both residential mobility and the incremental housing processes. This entire analysis is based on a primary survey of 933 households, statistically selected so as to yield direct estimates for the city.

Chapter Two critically examines India's housing policies. It is shown that there has been a gradual recognition that it would be worthwhile for the public sector to move away from direct construction of houses and to rely on indirect measures to influence the pattern of supply. This review of housing policy also establishes the need to evolve strategies at the local level which recognise the patterns of housing need, demand and supply in the specific urban context.

An analysis of supply processes is presented in Chapters Three and Four. Chapter Three provides an overview of the growth of the city population, economy and housing situation. Chapter Four examines in detail the contribution of various segments of suppliers and the factors influencing their behaviour.

An analysis of the housing demand in Ahmedabad is presented in Chapter Five. Estimates of income and price elasticities are presented for tenure and income classes. This chapter also presents the results of hedonic analysis identifying the important housing attributes and their share in determining the market price.

Chapters Six and Seven report our findings on the preference structure of different household groups and their housing adjustment processes. Chapter Six also examines the constraints faced by various household groups in attaining the preferred housing characteristics. Chapter Eight has a discussion on intra-urban mobility and incremental housing as modes of housing adjustment. A synthesis of households' preferences, constraints and adjustment processes is presented through stylised typologies in the concluding part of this chapter. The final chapter summarises the important findings of the study and highlights some of the policy directions.

2. *Urban Housing Policies in India*

In a planned economy like India, the government has the responsibility of ensuring provision of basic needs such as food, shelter and clothing at socially justifiable levels. While significant progress has been made to ensure provision of food, the shelter front is witnessing a worsening situation. Urban housing, in particular, which is plagued by both shortages and distributional problems, has now become an important area of public concern.

This concern is primarily due to the fact that in successive national plans, the housing sector has received a lower priority each time. The overall investment in housing declined from a very high 34 per cent in the First Five Year Plan to a mere 7.4 per cent in the Sixth Five Year Plan, with a public sector outlay at a mere 1.5 per cent. The relative share of resources for housing in the total budget has thus dwindled to an alarmingly low figure. While the larger allocation of planned resources across various sectors of the national economy may be justified with reference to a shift in Plan objectives, the housing sector is relegated to the background in recent plans as it is probably regarded as a non-productive sector by the planners.

The planners may have been influenced by the fact that compared to the overall performance of the economy, manifested by a steady growth in investment and capital formation, the housing sector presents a distressing picture. For instance, the percentage share of housing in the National Income is only about 4 per cent which has, in fact, declined slightly in the last two decades. The growth rate of the gross capital stock in housing has been only about 1.5 to 1.6 per cent per annum and the total investment in housing has declined from about 4 per cent of Gross Domestic Product in 1950–51 to less than 2.5 per cent in the mid-seventies (Gupta, 1985).

While these declining trends are partly an indication of the attempts to diversify the country's industrial and resource base, they do represent a worsening housing situation. This is particularly true for the urban areas, where the population has grown rapidly in the last two decades with a gradual increase in the real per capita income. These factors are, in fact, conducive to a rapid increase in the demand for housing. However, this increase has not been met, due to supply constraints related to certain legislative controls like rent control, land ceiling and limited housing finance. Our specific concern here is with the housing situation of the urban poor which has progressively worsened over the last two decades. Whether one looks at the situation in aggregate terms at the national level or at the city level, the evidence overwhelmingly points to a deterioration of the housing conditions. As will be seen from the analysis given in the next section, even the few indicators which have marked some improvement, those benefits have also disproportionately gone to the better-off sections of society.

Dynamics of the Housing Situation

The dynamics of the housing situation are reflected in the flow of services which accrue from a given housing stock and its temporal changes. These could be with respect to the quality of shelter, size, amenities, tenure and location. Though the real paucity of detailed data does not permit an indepth inquiry, an analysis of the available data reveals some important trends.

HOUSING STOCK AND CROWDING

In terms of mere availability of a house for each household, the situation has apparently improved over time, with the ratio of households per occupied dwelling unit having fallen from 1.24 in 1951 to 1.07 in 1981. This is combined with a fall in vacancy rate, which also decreased from 9.14 to 7.77 in 1981. Similarly, even in terms of the house size, the proportion of households in a one-room house has shown a slight decline in urban India and in all metropolitan cities except Delhi and Pune. However, these indicators may be deceptive as the slow growth of housing units, in relation to the population, has probably deferred household formation for many. As a result, crowding has increased, as seen in the rising persons per room ratio. This is even more serious in view of the fact that the existing average per capita floor space availability is low and is declining further especially in metropolitan cities where the average per capita floor space was only 6.11 sq.m.

and 67 per cent had less than 4.5 sq.m. per person. In urban India, it has declined from 7.86 sq.m. in 1953–54 to 6.89 sq.m. in 1973–74. Further, wide disparities prevail in terms of available floor space per person in relation to the income levels (Gupta, 1985).

HOUSING QUALITY AND AMENITIES

The building materials used reflect a significant improvement in the quality of shelter especially in the metropolitan areas. This probably camouflages the obsolescence taking place due to want of effective maintenance in some of the older stock. Although no detailed statistics are available, studies in some cities indicate that this proportion is probably around 20 per cent.

In terms of amenities, although the dependence on non-tap water sources has declined considerably, more than 75 per cent households in 1973–74 did not have exclusive water facilities. Similarly, 33.3 per cent of the households had no access to toilets, whereas 42.7 per cent had only shared facilities in 1973–74. Further, there has been little improvement in both these aspects over a period of time. Many studies have also revealed that actual conditions in most of the shared facilities is abysmally poor due to lack of proper maintenance.

TENURE

No improvement has taken place in terms of house ownership over a period of time. The Census of India's Housing Tables of 1961 and 1971, reported that 47 per cent of urban households owned their own houses. In most metropolitan cities, there has even been a decline in proportion of households staying in owned houses. The only exception to this is Ahmedabad where it has increased from 17.6 in 1961 to 23.7 per cent in 1971 and 35.9 per cent in 1981. However, a more detailed look indicates that these gains have accrued only to relatively better-off income groups. The lower income groups are severely constrained in becoming house owners in the formal sector.

The tenure issue is better visible in the mushrooming growth of slums in most urban areas. The proportion of slum population is generally much higher in larger cities where the question of a secure tenure for these households has plagued most local authorities.

The picture that emerges is one of partial improvement in the quality of shelter but with greater deterioration in terms of crowding, environmental conditions and the legal aspects of the housing situation, especially for the lower strata of the population. Whether this situation reflects a failure of the planned efforts for housing is analysed through a review of the evolution of housing policies in India in the following section.

Evolution of Housing Policies

PRE-INDEPENDENCE DEVELOPMENTS

Most attempts at planned intervention in housing began only after 1947. In pre-independence India there were not even rhetorical attempts oriented to the housing problems, especially of the disadvantaged groups. However, two important developments during the colonial rule influenced the residential patterns in free India. The first is with reference to programmes and measures favouring the elite (both the colonial and indigenous) and at times the even wilful neglect of other indigenous areas which led to a policy of deliberate residential segregation. The British brought to India their notions of town planning as reflected in building comfortable residential accommodation, wide roads, large open spaces and low density urban sprawl (Gilbert and Gugler, 1982). They used these principles in areas which were planned and constructed largely for their own use. Unfortunately, the egalitarian basis underlying these principles in their evolutionary context in the West, were totally absent in their applications on the Indian soil. In contrast, the pre-existing or new indigenous housing areas for the lower strata were neglected or given less emphasis and resources. The elite and upper middle classes benefited from the only financial assistance available for housing. These patterns are clearly visible in most Indian cities in their distinctly segregated residential areas.

The second other major development which has had a lasting effect on the housing situation is the legislation regarding restrictions on rent and tenancy which followed the Bombay Rent Restriction Act in 1939. Although initiated as 'adhoc emergency measures to prevent war profiteering by landlords in areas of acute housing shortages', these have persisted to the present day (Gupta 1985). None of the state governments have gathered enough political will to amend this legislation which has presumably led to disrepair in the old rental stock, inequities to different groups of tenants, a probable reduction in supply of formal rental housing, losses to the public exchequer and the operation of a parallel (black) housing market.

STANDARD SHELTER AND THE TECHNOLOGY PARADIGM

The major change in the housing perspective after independence came with a recognition that the public sector must play a direct and positive role. The egalitarian rhetoric of the early days of independence also prevailed in the sphere of housing as reflected in this quote from the First Five Year Plan: 'The private enterprise is not in a position to do the job so far as the low income groups are concerned. They cannot afford to pay the economic rent for housing accommodation of even the minimum standards' (Planning Commission, 1952).

The basic problem was thus recognised as an economic one, in terms of a gap between affordabilities and housing costs. The major underlying premise of this approach has, however, been the concept of a 'standard' quality, which in the earlier days was largely linked to the notion of an acceptable quality of shelter, in terms of size and building materials. The first response to this was recourse to a technology paradigm, which could reduce the gap between costs and affordabilities, using technological alternatives for low-cost housing. Secondly, throughout the fifties the Government of India had initiated a number of different social housing schemes through the Five Year Plans. These basically reflected a target group approach to provide an acceptable quality of shelter to disadvantaged occupational groups and lower income strata of population. Subsidies and loans were made available to different local authorities to provide housing through these schemes. The third component in this approach was related to the slum clearance and relocation attempts. The slums were identified basically with reference to the physical condition of shelter and at times with the illegality of the tenure. The attempt was to rehouse the slum dwellers in highly subsidised and standard quality shelter after demolishing their earlier slum dwellings.

These processes were initiated through the central sector in the decade following independence. The next decade saw almost all the schemes transferred to the state sector. Variations of old schemes with a range of ceiling costs, patterns of assistance and criteria for selecting beneficiaries along with a number of new schemes were introduced by different state governments. However, the basic approach throughout the sixties did not undergo any substantial change. In the meanwhile, the inadequacies of the housing programmes were gradually recognised both by the academicians/researchers and the public sector planners and implementers.

In terms of the technology paradigm, the earlier emphasis on industrialised building systems proved quite futile. To quote Strassman (1975):

> First, time savings in the house production are illusionary for it frequently takes as long to set up the complex systems as to undertake conventional dwellings. Second, the cost reductions are likely to be offset by formidable transport costs to the site. Third, due to high fixed costs, volume production is mandatory, inevitable bottlenecks at critical points in the operation will cause costs to skyrocket. Excluding land, industrialised systems building cannot reduce structural costs by more than ten to fifteen per cent while it can easily double or triple them . . . if things go wrong.

In recognition of such findings, the national level research institutions like Central Building Research Institution (CBRI), Roorkee, have slowly started shifting emphasis to developing techniques using indigenous technology and materials. It is slowly being recognised that improved and innovative techniques in use of mud, unburnt bricks, lime plaster and development of indigenous sanitation systems for better efficiency and standardisation can yield better results.

With respect to the target group approach of the social housing schemes, the four walls notion of standard shelter has turned this entire attempt into a drop in the ocean. On the one hand, the cost of even the cheapest house built under these schemes was beyond the means of the target groups. In Ahmedabad, almost two-thirds of the population was unable to afford the cheapest standard quality house.* On the other hand, this entailed heavy subsidisation and limited the effective reach of the programme in relation to

---

* A World Bank Study estimated that 64 per cent of households in Ahmedabad and 63 per cent in Madras were unable to afford the cheapest dwellings presently available in selected cities. See World Bank (1975).

both the needs and requirements. Further, due to leakages both in allocation (because of faulty selection procedures) and in subsequent subletting and turnover, the real benefits of the public sector provision and subsidies have, to a large extent, accrued to households outside the target groups. The public acceptance of this failure is evident in the Fourth Plan which conceded that the unit cost in public housing programmes was very high and with the constraint on resources, it was not possible for the public sector programmes to touch even the fringe of the housing problem.

The slum clearance and the subsequent relocation attempts in the sixties also met the same fate to a large extent. The whole approach required heavy subsidisation. The limited success of such a programme and its reasons were recognised in the early sixties itself. The third Plan identified the reasons as lengthy and cumbersome procedures involved in land acquisition, non-availability and high cost of alternative sites near existing slums, inability of slum dwellers to pay even the subsidised rent and their reluctance to move from the areas selected for clearance. This approach also failed to recognise the investments made by the people and caused unbearable hardships on the groups who were already being deprived in other spheres of activities.* Besides these specific problems, the major drawback of this approach was its extremely limited reach in relation to the needs.

PLANNING LESSONS AND NEW POLICY PERSPECTIVES

The evolution of planning in any sphere of activity can be regarded as a learning process, in order that the earlier efforts and its impact, gradually lead to incremental changes in the planning approach. The analysis of the results in India and the experiences of researchers and administrators in the field of housing in other developing countries have contributed to the learning process in planning for housing. The important lessons may be summarised as follows:

The high costs of providing standard quality shelter and the related need for high levels of subsidies implied that the effective reach of ublic housing schemes would be very limited. This aspect gradually

---

* There are innumerable such attempts which have been recorded. For one of the more well reported incidents, see Deshpande (1976).

gained more importance in view of the rising costs of construction and decreasing rate of resources allocated for housing.

There was a gradual recognition of the importance of other housing aspects especially for the lower income groups. It was slowly understood that the benefits accruing from better levels of infrastructure, and improved forms of tenure are far greater than those from 'pucca' shelter in our temperate climates. The middle class values, attached to the four walls notion of housing, was slowly undergoing a change.

Twenty years of technological research clearly indicated its limited role in reducing the cost-affordability gap. On the other hand, the houses built and managed by the people or communities themselves were far cheaper than any of those provided by the public schemes.

The process of housing supply was seen to comprise different activities and levels of action, each of which demanded different scales and kinds of organisation along with different mixes of skill. Each level of action, therefore, offered varying opportunities for participation. Of the three major activities related to housing, it was felt that the assemblies of different elements and components must be done by the household or community at the local level, while the central level should concentrate on legislative controls to limit the concentration of resources and ensure local access to resources. The municipal level may focus on the provision of components. This assertion is based on findings which indicated that the processes with locally assembled housing not only offer economies of scale but are also likely to satisfy the highly variable priorities of the users. On the other hand, most types of infrastructure and public services are more efficiently handled at the settlement level.*

Matching the concept of 'self-help' discussed above, housing was explained as a process rather than a mere packaged product—a verb rather than a noun. The main emphasis was on the need side for understanding the preferences and priorities for various housing attributes or services in a dynamic perspective. On the supply side, the emphasis was on disaggregating the housing process into different stages. The major emphasis was on the

---

* John Turner has been the pioneer in developing these concepts. See Turner (1976).

popular sector which presumably developed housing for its own consumption. Housing was, therefore, seen not so much as a commodity in the market place but in terms of the use value it represented for the user.

The investment rate in housing over the different plan periods has shown a consistent decline. This is also true of the private sector investment. One of the major constraints faced in urban India was a lack of an effective housing finance structure with the necessary intermediaries. It was gradually being recognised that greater stimulus was necessary to attract more private sector investment into housing.

These different lessons pointed towards two new policy perspectives. Firstly, the emerging trend is towards support policies which provide the necessary housing services and ensure access to elements which promote local action. This is in direct contrast to the earlier centrally administered programmes which substitute for activities that are better controlled locally. The second major difference in the policy perspective is the acceptance of the progressive model of development which essentially focuses on the provision of a secure tenure and a range of basic services. It is expected that these will enable and encourage low-income households to improve their housing structures through self-help financing and/or construction. The two main types of projects envisaged under this model are sites and services and slum upgradation projects which are integrated urban projects rather than mere conventional public housing projects. This approach is more commonly referred to as the 'self-help' approach which relies on the low-income households' own initiatives to assemble the resources to produce housing.

SEVENTIES: A DECADE OF CHANGES

True to the new conceptions of planning as 'a learning process' these new outlooks and perspectives are clearly reflected in the change in housing programmes initiated in the seventies which was a very eventful one as compared to the sixties. The major changes in policy perspectives have come in three specific directions. Firstly, with reference to the programmes related to slum areas, the emphasis has decisively shifted from the former clearance and large scale relocation policies towards environmental improvement. The second major direction of change has come in the form of the recognition of the importance of housing finance and setting up of specialised organisations for this purpose. Lastly, the rhetoric on the importance of land policies heard throughout the sixties finally resulted in the form of specific measures related to land for housing.

Although the importance of the improvement measures rather than clearance and relocation was always accepted in principle, it was only with the massive Bustee Improvement Scheme in Calcutta, with a hundred per cent central grant, that the central sector scheme of Environmental Improvement of Slums came effectively into force in 1972. The recent Task Force set up by the Planning Commission aptly summarises the main factors which were responsible in ushering this change. These include 'widespread resentment from the people against large scale demolition of established communities under the slum clearance programme; an increase in the funds required for such a programme compared with the availability of limited resources; rapid deterioration of the "fit" structures; the changes in emphasis was expected to induce owners to undertake renovation of properties; and it was expected that a large number of slum dwellers could be benefited within the given resources, if improvement of slums was resorted to' (Planning Commission, 1983). The scheme has gradually been extended to all urban areas in the country. The basic aim is to provide certain minimum amenities which are crucial for improving the environmental conditions. Despite this rational basis, several problems have emerged in the actual implementation of the scheme.

Most importantly, the entire approach has been overtly oriented to fulfilling financial targets. Quite often, the amenities provided are both inadequate and of poor quality. Further a total lack of participation by the people often leads to an imbalanced provision, which is either socially unsuitable or loaded in favour of the more influential leaders. Reluctance and neglect on the part of the local authorities and the lack of commitment from the people have often led to extremely poor maintenance. Most authorities have shied away from providing security of tenure to the slum-dwellers which may alone bring in the commitment necessary for effective maintenance of these amenities. Further, the improvement of shelter is also crucially linked to the question of tenure.

The second major change during the seventies came with the setting up of the Housing and Urban Development Corporation (HUDCO), in response to the need of housing agencies for long-term housing finance. Although HUDCO has fulfilled an important need, its operations have been linked to constructions undertaken essentially by public sector organisations. Almost 98 per cent of its financing has been allocated to different public sector agencies for specific public housing projects. Its finances are 'targeted for particular type of dwelling units with restrictions on the plinth area, overall cost and income classification of the beneficiaries'. It was only in 1977, with the setting up of the Housing Development and Finance Corporation (HDFC) that long-term housing finance was made available to the private sector. HDFC, is, therefore, emerging as a major financial institution, comparable with the savings and loan associations in the USA and building societies in Britain.

Despite these innovations in housing finance, two important problems still remain. Firstly, except for HDFC, most other housing finance bodies are far too rigidly linked to the direct construction activity by public sector agencies. Secondly, these new avenues for housing finance completely ignore the needs of the lower income groups. Their specific preferences for smaller amounts and recurring loans, flexible loan repayment schedules and a more responsive and adaptive machinery for giving and recovering loans are not generally possible to satisfy within the confines of conventional financing institutions. Despite the fact that on paper almost 85 per cent of HUDCO financed housing was meant for the economically weaker sections (EWS) and lower income groups (LIG), in reality large-scale leakages exist in these projects. Thus, within the area of housing finance, it is clearly necessary to devise ways to mobilise private resources and make concrete attempts to reach the relatively lower strata of the population.

As early as the Third Five Year Plan, special emphasis was laid on 'land acquisition and development as the key factors in the success of the housing programmes'. The committee set up to look into the need and directions for urban land policy had also given its report in 1964. It underlined 'the need for a long term urban level policy with particular emphasis on optimum social use of urban land, provision of adequate serviced land at reasonable prices, preventing concentration of land ownership and safeguarding the interests of the poor sections of the society' (Government of India, 1964). Despite this recognition, barring the case of large scale land acquisition by the Delhi Development Authority (DDA), no real emphasis can be observed through actual programmes related to this issue. It was only during the seventies that a large number of urban development authorities were set up some of which conducted bulk land acquisition. No evidence is so far available on the performance of these agencies. However, if one were to go by the evaluation of DDA's operations, the success of these measures is at best questionable. Despite the financial success of DDA, it has been unable to 'develop and release in time, adequate supply of serviced land'. The major lacuna has been the ineffective 'management capacity commensurate with the needs of large scale land development . . . there has hardly been any serious attempt to assess the land requirements of EWS and LIG, their affordability and the needs and possibilities of cross-subsidy'. On the whole then, the land banking function of DDA has been reduced to a 'mere commercial venture' (Datta, n.d.).

The other significant effort has been the launching of the sites and services schemes with the Sixth Five Year Plan, recognising the need for 'direct public sector assistance for housing the EWS with emphasis on sites and services schemes'. The more important of the sites and services type projects have been Delhi's Resettlement Colonies Project, Hyderabad Urban Community Development Project, Arumbakkam Sites and Services Project at Madras and Vasna Resettlement Project at Ahmedabad. 'These projects differ vastly from each other in approach, focus, size and impact, with the Delhi project being closer to the conventional emphasis on sites and services and the Vasna project on the other end of the spectrum', with the provision of a minimal dwelling structure (Datta, n.d.). The emphasis also varied in terms of the levels of amenities and the extent of cost recovery and cross subsidisation attempted. Although not many evaluative studies are available for these recent projects, a few observations clearly point towards possible future courses of action. First, the importance of security of tenure is clearly evident from these projects. However, there are other constraints to shelter development foremost of which could be the low affordability for shelter and lack of financial assistance. This problem will be further enhanced if the programme expands significantly and reaches the lower strata. People are also often unwilling to build due to the demonstration effect of having seen the publicly provided 'pucca dwellings'. Several problems are also related to the concept of 'affordability' and the later cost recovery of loans. The more important ones are:

— Variable nature of income of the lower strata along with the need to remit money 'home'.
— The ability and willingness to pay for housing does not depend merely on income, as assumed in most other projects.
— The importance of other variables like social background, stage in life cycle, educational and occupational backgrounds and tenure, are not adequately considered.
— Demonstration effect of other highly subsidised housing leads to formation of pressure groups demanding concessions in payments.
— Often, the repayment schedule is equated directly with the affordability, without keeping provision for cost incurred in the construction and maintenance of shelter (Planning Commission, 1983).

A related issue is the locational pattern of these projects. The high priority attached to employment accessibility by lower income groups is quite rational. If these projects fail to respond to this preference, they may worsen the economic conditions of these groups.* These observations suggest that, despite the obvious potential, unless the sites and services approach is firmly linked to an overall urban housing strategy, it may remain confined to a few show-piece projects only.

These recent developments indicate certain contradictions in the entire approach to the policies for urban housing in India. On the one hand, there is a recognition of the self-help approach and the need for support policies rather than the earlier substitution policies. At the same time, most housing boards and other housing agencies continue to allocate a major share of the resources for regular public housing projects. Secondly, despite the recognition of the need for slum improvement, slum clearance and demolition drives

* There are many examples of households which move back to their original sites due to inconvenient locations. For example, see the reflections on Vasna Project in Planning Commission (1983). Further, other studies of urban labour market also suggest that location plays a crucial role in determining access to better employment opportunities and incomes even for workers who are otherwise comparable (c.f. Mehta, 1982 and Swamy, 1983).

continue unabated, sometimes even with renewed vigour. These contradictions point to the conflicting attitudes of planners and academicians and the fact that housing policies are dependent on political forces as much or even more than the technical solutions that it represents.

Gilbert and Gugler (1982) explain the contradiction in terms of the mutually conflicting interests of different elite groups (class fractions). The state is subject to pressure from representatives of various capitalist groups. Its housing response, therefore, constitutes a balance between these demands. Thus, national governments may respond to industrial interests, vaguely sympathetic to spontaneous settlement, because of the cheap labour force it offers, by failing to formulate a consistent housing policy or by supporting self-help programmes. Meanwhile local government policy may respond to the pressure from elite residential groups and the construction industry whose best interests are served by demolition and slum clearance. Such local action would be favoured when the poor have occupied high value land awaiting development, when they have blocked prestigious public works programmes, and when the poor have established themselves close to middle and upper income housing areas, thus threatening to lower land and property values.

Thus, the slum improvement programme promoted by national and industrial political influences is at times counterbalanced by the more local political forces, especially supported by the lobby of large land owners and private housing and estate developers. At times the local government may also accept the slums, due to their sheer incapacity to handle the problem by actually providing better houses. Thus, both the slum clearance and improvement and the other unauthorised developments indicate the underlying political processes, besides the techno-economic aspects of rising prices and unaffordabilities.

Alternative Paradigms

What then are the directions for the future which emerge from this review of evolution of housing policies in India? The past efforts clearly point to the need to recognise the importance of incorporating feedback to guide future actions. While realising that there cannot be any simplistic solutions to the complex problem of housing, certain alternative lines of action do emerge. These represent both the outlooks which are already emerging on the housing scene in India and the changes which appear essential in the planning approach.

One of the most important changes in approach relates to the need to think beyond direct house construction and direct intervention by the public sector. It is clearly evident that the public sector may do well to focus on more indirect methods which will affect the housing supply so that it is more responsive to the housing needs of all income groups. Often, many of the indirect measures in the past have inadvertently added to the list of constraints, instead of limiting and removing them. Prime candidates for revision include urban land policy, rent control and housing and land development standards set by development control rules. Further, other indirect measures like land taxation, land price monitoring system, granting of land tenure and legal aid can also be used effectively to guide the supply of land which must form the basic element in any housing strategy. Similarly, innovations in the housing finance system, directed to delink it from direct construction and channel its flow to the lower strata of the population are also urgently necessary.

A second aspect of change in the approach to planning is the need to evolve housing policy perspectives at the state and local urban area level. Under the Indian Constitution, housing falls in the State list. Direct central assistance for social housing schemes was available to the States in the earlier Plans, but since the Fourth Five Year Plan, these have been replaced by block grants. The responsibility of ensuring adequate housing thus essentially rests with the State and local governments. However, despite this need to revise the existing legislative measures and controls at the State and local level, most of the local governments are content to adopt the national level 'model' Acts without any modifications. While such an approach obviously implies a path of least action by the local governments, it is also due to a lack of adequate understanding about the local housing markets.

An understanding of the local housing market becomes even more crucial in the light of the gradual acceptance of the housing support policies approach. The local governments today do not maintain an adequate information base to assess the housing condition of its residents. If these agencies are expected to play a positive role in generating a climate which is conducive even for the private sector to cater to the housing needs of the urban poor, then in addition to the basic information, these agencies will also have to understand the local market in terms of the supply process and the residential choice behaviour. The present research has been carried out within this perspective.

3. Population, Economy and Housing in Ahmedabad

Ahmedabad is often cited as a 'success story' of cooperative housing movement in the country. Subsequently, the private commercial sector, has become dominant in the housing sector. The housing activity in the city is closely related to the economic growth and decline of the city.

Ahmedabad's major contribution to the national economy has been through its textile industry, which is why it is often referred to as the 'Manchester of India'. However, in recent years Ahmedabad has faced problems both on the economic and socio-political fronts. The textile industry has suffered stagnation and even outright closures. The situation has been aggravated by continuing problems of intermittent rioting and communal tensions in the city during the last two decades. However, Ahmedabad's resilience to such problems in the past, will hopefully stand by it in the future.

Changing Economic Fortunes

Ahmedabad was founded on the banks of river Sabarmati by Sultan Ahmed Shah in 1411 AD. 'Ahmedabad's story is of the survival and transformation of an important traditional centre of trade and industry into a modern industrial city, under the leadership of an indigenous financial and mercantile elite.' (Gillion, 1968).

From the time of its inception, Ahmedabad flourished for almost three centuries despite the severe famines which often rocked it. The eighteenth century, however, saw a decline of the city with repeated natural calamities and the disorderly and opportunistic rule of the Maratha rulers. Even during this phase, the pragmatic mercantile elite survived and during the relative security of the British rule brought back the past glory.

The major change, however, came towards the end of the nineteenth century with a rapid rise of the textile industry. The mercantile elite, with their surplus capital, used this industry as an avenue for profitable investments.* The city's economy was further affected by the First World War. The stoppage of textile goods from England gave a remarkable impetus to the local textile industry. This was further supported by the Swadeshi movement of 1921 started by Mahatma Gandhi. Thus, for the first time after the war, Ahmedabad's textile products entered into competition with foreign goods. This was reflected in a rise both in the number of textile units and employment.

The textile industry underwent subtle structural changes during the decades preceding 1947. The renewed competition with foreign textiles led to an improvement in the quality of textile goods produced in the local mills. The number of functioning units, however, did not greatly increase in the forties, as many mills with outdated machinery were forced to close down. The employment numbers, however, rose steadily, reaching almost 1,25,000 workers in 1950.

The last three decades have witnessed considerable change in the economic structure of the city. The dominant and dynamic textile industry has more or less stagnated with no growth in employment and even some absolute decline. The conditions have worsened considerably during the eighties with almost 25 units closing down, leaving about 50,000 workers without any job opportunities (Sen, 1988).

A closer look at the city's economic structure will identify the major trends, most prominent of which is the stagnation in the formal manufacturing sector in the city.

STRUCTURE AND GROWTH OF ORGANISED AND UNORGANISED SECTORS IN AHMEDABAD

Ahmedabad's economy can be broadly understood if a distinction is made between its organised and unorganised sectors. However, this task is considerably hampered by the paucity of data in the required form. There are only two potential sources which give comprehensive information for the organised sector. One is the

* Sompura (1983) cites several reasons for the existence of surplus capital. These include 'contraction of former outlets in money lending to princes and armies, a restriction of the opium trade, decline of their insurance business with better security under the British and the competition from branches of English banks' (p. 34).

Directorate of Employment and Training which collects and publishes data under the Employment Market Information Scheme (EMI), for all public and private sector establishments which employ more than 25 persons since 1961. Although this data applies to the entire Ahmedabad district, it indicates trends for the city with reasonable accuracy, since the contribution of the Ahmedabad Urban Agglomeration was as high as 83 per cent in the non-agricultural workforce of Ahmedabad district in the year 1981.

Using this data base, it is possible to determine the importance of organised and unorganised labour in major industry divisions. The primary activities fall almost totally outside the scope of the organised sector. On the other hand, more than two-thirds of the workers engaged in manufacturing, construction and utilities are in the organised sector. Unlike popular notions, a substantial number of workers, even in manufacturing, are also in the unorganised sector. They constitute almost one-third of the total workers in the unorganised sector.

At the aggregate level, the work-force is almost equally divided between the two sectors, Papola's (1978) estimate based on establishment tables of the Census, and using a more liberal measure, (establishments employing ten and more workers as organised sector) gave an estimated 55 per cent of the work-force in the unorganised sector in 1971. This is compatible with our estimates of 50 per cent for Ahmedabad district. In any case, it is most probable that half the work-force in Ahmedabad is in the unorganised sector. Within this sector, almost 60 per cent are own-account or independent workers, or unpaid family workers. The rest are employees in small establishments.

The employment in the organised sector in Ahmedabad district grew by about 3.5 per cent per annum from 1961 to 1971. In fact, in the first half of the decade it grew at a fairly high rate of 3.6 per cent per annum but came down to a little less than 3 per cent in the latter part of the decade. The seventies saw a further decline in the growth rate of organised employment, which was only 2 per cent per annum in the first half. It went up to 2.7 per cent per annum in the second half. Over the twenty year period, the unorganised sector employment grew at 4.1 per cent per annum as compared to the 3.3 per cent growth for the organised sector. Thus, the unorganised sector absorbed almost 70 per cent of the growth in employment. However, the declining trend of organised sector growth at just 2.5 per cent per annum in the 1971–81 decade, is more alarming. The seriousness of the situation in the urban economy of Ahmedabad is evident from the fact that there is an almost stagnant situation in the manufacturing sector. The growth of tertiary sector is also mainly in the public sector. The structure of these patterns are, therefore, examined in further detail.

The growth of public sector employment is a major feature of organised employment growth in both the decades. Although the private sector still remains the larger employer, the employment in public sector rose at 88.3 and 42.9 per cent respectively as compared to 19.8 and 15.8 per cent growth in private sector during the two decades. There are two factors which have contributed to this growth of the public sector. The first is merely statistical and does not represent a growth in overall employment. This is because of the bank nationalisation in 1969 which resulted in the transfer of bank employees to the public sector. However, even if adjusted for this shift, the total public sector organised employment rose by 64 per cent as against the private sector growth rate of 26.3 per cent for 1961–71 decade. The second major source of growth in public sector employment during this decade may have been due to the formation of Gujarat State which brought about an expansion of government administration in both the central and state level departments.

Stagnation of Manufacturing Employment

Table A 3.1 clearly brings out the picture of stagnation in manufacturing. Not only did its proportion to total employment in the organised sector fall in 1961–71 decade, but even in absolute terms it recorded the lowest growth rate of a mere 1 per cent per annum. Although in the last decade it has picked up again by returning a growth rate of 2.3 per cent per annum, in proportional terms it remains at the same level. As more than half the work-force in the organised sector is in manufacturing, its fortunes are likely to have a great impact on the total employment in it.

A large proportion of the manufacturing division is employed in the textile industry. About 80 per cent of the work-force in Ahmedabad city, and about 68 per cent in the rest of district who were engaged in manufacturing were in the textile industry. Over the last two decades, this major industry has seen an absolute decline in employment. There was a 'replacement of men by machinery'. As pointed out by Joshi and Joshi (1976) for Bombay, this was.

> probably, in part, a case of pure factor substitution in response to higher wage costs but probably also reflects changes in techniques in response to changing product-mix and also pure technical progress. Superior techniques tend to involve increases in capital intensity and so do new types of cloth-synthetics and blends—as well as higher quality cotton textiles (p. 63).

This is borne out by the ASI data for the Census sector for Ahmedabad city. Although the fixed capital in textiles grew by 86.8 per cent in the period 1960–69 and the output by 88 per cent, the employment in large-scale textile units fell by 13.9 per cent during the same period.

In the district as a whole, which includes the new developments on Ahmedabad's eastern periphery, notably Odhav, Vatwa and Naroda, engineering industries have grown much faster. The share of this industry in the total manufacturing employment has gone up to 14.4 per cent in 1980. Both chemicals and non-metallic mineral products also contribute about 3.6 per cent to the manufacturing work-force in the district. It must be pointed out that more than 33 per cent of the units in these industries employ less than 25 workers, as compared to less than 20 per cent for textiles. It is quite likely that the working conditions and earnings of workers in these units are not comparable to the textile workers. Thus, in terms of earning opportunities for workers in Ahmedabad there has probably been a decline over the last two decades.

GROWTH OF TERTIARY SECTOR

Ahmedabad's economy seems to present a case of tertiarisation, as is evident from both the Census and EMI data. During the sixties, the importance of this sector has increased. It is, however, necessary to check whether the growth of the tertiary sector has resulted from absorption in the so-called informal sector or whether it represents a dynamic evolution. Even within the organised sector, the growth may have resulted from external factors like the formation of the state of Gujarat rather than being truly demand based. The scanty evidence available presents a mixed picture. Although some of the tertiary sector growth is clearly absorptive in character, an equally important proportion is probably demand based.

Within the tertiary division which employed almost 30 per cent of the organised sector workers, the fastest growing division has been trade and commerce which increased almost four times over the two decades. A substantial portion of this is in the finance and commerce division in 1981. The largest proportion, however, is in other services which covers administration, education, health etc. Thus, it is the relatively higher educated labour which has been absorbed in the organised part of the tertiary sector.

On the whole then, despite the moderate growth in population and labour force, the organised sector in Ahmedabad has failed to keep pace. In 1971, the share of the organised sector in the total work-force was about 50 per cent which was an increase of 3.8 per cent from its share in 1961. However, in 1981, the share has actually declined by almost 5.5 per cent. Although manufacturing is the predominant activity in the organised sector, the share of tertiary activities at 30 per cent is also not insignificant. Further, the tertiary activities, especially in the public sector, are gaining importance whereas the manufacturing employment mainly in the textile industry has stagnated in the last two decades. Thus, there has been a worsening of opportunities in the organised sector.

Despite these downward trends, Ahmedabad continues to be an important centre. According to a recent study, it contributed to the extent of 16.3 per cent of the total income and 28.5 per cent of the industrial income of the State in 1976–77 (Kashyap, 1984). However, the fruits of these developments and even the ill-effects of Ahmedabad's misfortunes have been distributed very unevenly across the various socio-economic classes in the city. This is evident as the lowest 50 per cent of the households earn only 20 per cent of the total labour income while the top decile gets almost one-third of the total income.

Population, Migration and Residential Mobility

According to India's first official census, Ahmedabad had a population of 1,20,000 in 1872. After about six decades of moderate growth, the population had almost doubled between 1931–41. Since then, Ahmedabad's growth rate has been moderate compared to other Indian metropolises. The last decade (1971–81) even indicates a slightly downward trend. Spatially over the last three decades, the population has moved outwards from within the fort walls and the saturated inner areas to the peripheral areas.

The changing economic fortunes in the city are also reflected in the patterns of migration. Net migrants, both in proportion to total population and their share in the total population growth, have remained stable in the seventies, suggesting that a large part of the city's growth may be attributed to a natural increase only. Ahmedabad, of course, is no exception to general conditions in metropolitan India. Many researchers have observed that this is true for most of the metropolises in India (Mitra et al. 1980 and Mukherjee and Banerjee, 1978). Along with declining opportunities in Ahmedabad, the importance of other cities in Gujarat has increased—all indicating significantly higher growth rates. The decline in net migration does not merely indicate a slow-down in migration to Ahmedabad but even a substantial out-migration. Crude analysis of available data suggests out-migration of over 1,00,000 persons from Ahmedabad during the seventies.*

In 1971, about 45 per cent of Ahmedabad's population comprised of migrants which had reduced to 38 per cent in 1981. Migrants have a bulging age-sex pyramid at working age groups in all the three census years suggesting that adult migrants come to Ahmedabad after growing up in their native places. A low sex-ratio in 1961 and 1971 may imply that male migrants come without their wives at least in the initial years. The dramatic increase in sex-ratio in 1981, however, suggests rising pattern of household consolidation.

INTRA-URBAN MOBILITY

Migration within an intra-urban perspective presents some interesting results. Although the rates of residential mobility as revealed by our study are very low, some clear trends of movements are evident through simultaneous examination of aggregate and household level data. The area within the fort walls, popularly known as the walled city shows a clearly stabilising trend. From 1961 to 1971, there has been only marginal increase in population, while

* On the basis of information on the duration of residence of migrants, about 3,32,000 persons must have come to the Ahmedabad Urban Agglomeration during the 61–71 decade. In comparison with the estimate of about 1,94,000 net migrants, this indicates an out-migration of almost 1,14,000 persons during this decade.

TABLE 3.1
Spatial Patterns of Population Growth in Ahmedabad Urban Area

Spatial Unit		1951	1961	1971	1981
1.	Ahmedabad Urban Agglomeration (AUA)	927,298	1,260,210 (35.6)	1,809,140 (43.5)	2,548,057 (40.8)
2.	Ahmedabad Municipal Corporation (AMC)	849,797	1,153,711 (35.8)	1,606,165 (39.2)	2,059,725 (28.2)
3.	AMC fort walls (AMCFW)	393,941	459,535 (16.8)	480,735 (4.6)	474,225 (−1.4)
4.	Outside the fort walls	455,856	694,176 (52.3)	1,125,430 (62.1)	2,585,500 (40.9)
	a. East (AMCE)	n.a.	555,964	856,525 (54.1)	1,153,043 (34.6)
	b. West (AMCW)	n.a.	138,212	268,905 (94.6)	432,457 (60.8)
5.	Agglomerated Periphery (AP)	70,110	106,499 (37.2)	202,975 (90.6)	458,332 (125.8)
	a. East (APE)	n.a.	89,819	167,461 (86.4)	349,367 (108.6)
	b. West (APW)	n.a.	16,680	35,514 (112.9)	138,965 (291.3)

Notes:
1. Figures in parenthesis are the decadal growth rates, adjusted for the changes in the boundary with 1981 as the base.
2. For AMC in 1951, 1961 and 1971, Danilimda is included as it is part of AMC in 1981.
3. For AUA, in 1951, 1961 and 1971 outgrowths of Maktampur, Shahwadi, Narol, Thaltej, Bodakdev, Ramol and Vatwa, Towns of Hansol, Nikol and villages of Shahijpurbaugha, Vejalpur, Vastrapur, Memnagar, Ghatlodiya, Ghodasar, Isanpur, Kali and Vatwa are included as they are part of AUA in 1981.

Sources:
1. For 1951, 1961 and 1971—*Census of India*, Series 5, Gujarat General Population Tables, Supplement to Part II-A, Table A-V, pp. 16–19.
2. For 1981—*Census of India*, Series 5, Gujarat, paper 2 of 1981, Final Population Tables.

the next decade even indicated an absolute decline in population. While population in the municipal area outside the fort walls grew rapidly during the sixties, seventies saw the growth shifting to the peripheries, particularly the western parts which witnessed a quadrupling of population during this decade.

A major factor for the 'depopulation' of the walled city is probably the high level of congestion and deterioration of residential environment with average densities of almost 1000 persons per hectare (pph) as compared to gross density of 100 pph for the entire Ahmedabad Urban Area and about 250 pph for the Ahmedabad Municipal Corporation. The occupancy rate, that is persons per residential unit, is also the highest in the walled city. It appears that the upper middle class sections of the population have changed their tastes for the residential environment with a high status attached to living in the upper income areas and in 'societies'. While during the pre-independence period such mobility processes were restricted to the elite, today the bulk of the households moving out belong to the upper middle class. The locational preference of these households appears to be largely in the west. Of the mobile households in western Ahmedabad, 40 per cent had moved from their initial residence in the walled city as compared to only 14 per cent for the eastern part of the city. There is very little residential movement into the walled city though the commercial activities still continue to be concentrated there. The high prices for such properties have also warded off many residential uses, resulting in use conversions.

On the whole then, almost two-thirds of the total households in the walled city have been living in the same house for over 30 years. Most of the remaining have also moved from within the walled city or represent new household formations. On the other hand, nearly 40 per cent of the households have stayed in the eastern peripheral areas for less than five years. Of the households moving into the east periphery from the rest of the city, 70 per cent have been from the eastern parts within the city. The eastern side of the city was inhabited rather early with the development of the textile mills as seen in the fact that almost 25 per cent of the households have been residents of the area for more than thirty years. However, it is still receiving additions and some turnover is probably also taking place through vacancies created by consolidating households moving to the eastern periphery. This is unlike the walled city, where the outward movement has not been replaced—as evident from the relatively high vacancy rates in the walled city.*

That the western parts of Ahmedabad were populated relatively recently is indicated by the fact that 75 to 90 per cent of the households have stayed there for less than 15 years, while the proportion of households who have never changed houses is not significantly different for areas outside the walled city. One of the

---

* Unfortunately, the data on spatial variations in vacancy rate is available for only 1961. However, micro studies in the walled city suggest high vacancy rates (cf Menon, 1985).

major reasons for this recent development of western Ahmedabad is the fact that a major part of the vacant land in this zone was originally held by a few elite groups who had the capacity to hold on to the land for speculative purposes. The town planning regulations under which town planning schemes (a land readjustment scheme) were prepared only ensured that the least amount of land area was to be used for building roads and for other public purposes. As a result, large undivided serviced plots were left with the land owners, who brought these lands in the market only during the 'boom' period of co-operative housing in the city. Through this, they could retain the elitist nature of the zone as they were selective in selling the land only to a particular class or caste group based cooperative housing society, as well as maintain a high profit margin.

TABLE 3.2
Spatial Patterns of Population and Housing Changes (1961–1981)

Spatial Units	Average Decadal Growth in Percentages					
	Population		Households		Housing Units	
	1961–71	1971–81	1961–71	1971–81	1961–71	1971–81
Ahmedabad Urban Agglomeration	43.5	40.8	35.1	39.7	40.8	40.7
Ahmedabad Municipal Corporation	39.2	28.2	29.5	25.2	34.1	26.1
Fort Walls	4.6	−1.4	−1.4	−3.3	2.7	−2.5
AMC Eastern	54.1	34.6	37.9	26.8	42.6	27.7
AMC Western	94.6	60.8	86.5	67.1	90.4	66.5
Agglomerated Periphery (Total)	90.6	125.8	96.5	114.8	129.4	147.1
A P Eastern	86.4	108.6	91.6	114.8	121.9	114.9
A P Western	112.9	291.3	121.9	278.6	121.9	299.7

Source: Computed from General Population Tables of Census, 1961, 1971, 1981.

On the whole, 65 per cent of the households in Ahmedabad have not changed their residence. During the five year span from 1979–84, only 7.3 per cent had moved once and another 1.1 per cent twice. The average mobility rate that emerges is only 1.7 per cent per annum which is very low in comparison with 10 per cent per annum in Australia (Seek, 1983) and other developed countries

TABLE 3.3
Duration of Residence by Zone of Residence and Tenure Status

Duration of Residence	Old City	AMCE	AMCW	East Periphery	West Periphery	Owners	Renters
Less than Five years	3.20	11.15	21.33	40.14	37.03	2.10	9.70
6 to 15 years	6.40	26.70	54.00	25.85	50.00	9.80	15.19
16 to 30 years	23.20	38.95	23.34	23.81	5.55	24.30	17.68
31 years or more	67.20	23.20	1.33	10.20	7.42	63.80	60.78
Total	100.00	100.00	100.00	100.00	100.00	100.00	100.00
	125	457	150	147	54	571	363

Note: Figures in the table are column percentages.

in the West. In addition to moving households, almost an equal proportion have probably set up households for the first time in Ahmedabad. This is surmised from the fact that compared to 8.4 per cent who have moved in the last five years, almost 18 per cent indicate a duration of stay in their current residence to be of less than five years. The intracity variation in the growth patterns and demographic structure are thus a reflection of both residential mobility as well as new household formation. While at an aggregate city level, population growth was greater than the rate of household formation, this was reversed in the peripheries, suggesting that a part of the growth in the newly developing peripheral areas was probably due to the formation of new households (Table 3.4).

Spatial Segmentation

On the whole, we find that the class-based spatial division of the city has strengthened over a period of time with selective movements of households in different areas. Today, Ahmedabad is almost literally divided by the Sabarmati river into rich and poor segments. The bulk of the earlier and recent growth in the east is by households belonging to the economically weaker sections. Their movement is also largely restricted to the eastern side. West Ahmedabad, which houses a majority of the better-off sections of society also has households at later stages in the life cycle and a larger proportion of owners. The walled city which still has a significant proportion of upper class households will probably

TABLE 3.4
Zone of Residence and Mobility

No of Moves since Household Formation	Old City	AMCE	AMCW	East Peri-phery	West Peri-phery	Total
No move	89.60	67.83	57.33	47.62	50.00	64.84
One	5.60	22.98	26.00	29.93	14.81	21.76
	(2.4)	(4.16)	(7.33)	(23.13)	(1.85)	(7.3)
Two	1.60	5.91	11.33	7.48	9.26	6.65
	(−)	(0.88)	(2.0)	(1.36)	(1.85)	(1.1)
More than two	3.20	1.09	2.00	10.20	12.95	3.64
	(−)	(−)	(−)	(−)	(−)	(−)
Total	125	457	150	147	54	933
	(100)	(100)	(100)	(100)	(100)	(100)

Note: 1. Cell values indicate column percentages.
2. The figures in parenthesis indicate mobility rate in the last five years.

undergo changes as these continue to move out west. Those who continue will probably be one's whose preference for low rents in the rent-controlled property outweigh the 'status' of a better house outside or those who lack an effective access to institutional finance.

This class-based segregation is reflected in the income-distribution patterns in different zones. There is a very clear clustering of specific income groups in different zones. On the whole almost 32 per cent of Ahmedabad households can be classified as economically weaker sections. However, this drops to less than twenty per cent in the walled city and the west, whereas rises to nearly 40 per cent in the eastern areas. Further, the richer householders are also more likely to be the owners, probably as they have a greater ability to pay the necessary down payments and/or have greater and easier access to institutional finance (Table 3.5).

Existing Housing Situation in Ahmedabad

At any given time, one of the most influencing factors with respect to the urban housing situation is the quality of the existing stock itself. The magnitude of new supply in a year generally does not exceed 4 to 5 per cent of the existing stock. Any understanding of the actual magnitude of the housing stock is severely hampered by

TABLE 3.5
Household Income Distribution by Zones

Zone	Monthly Household Income in Rupees					Total
	0 to 750	*751 to 1000*	*1000 to 1500*	*1500 to 2000*	*2000 and more*	
Old City	19.20	16.00	15.20	16.80	32.80	125 (100.0)
East AMC	37.85	15.54	19.04	10.50	17.07	457 (100.0)
West AMC	17.33	13.33	16.67	8.00	44.67	150 (100.0)
East Periphery	38.09	27.89	14.29	11.56	8.16	147 (100.0)
West Periphery	22.22	20.37	25.93	14.81	16.67	54 (100.0)
Total	31.19	17.47	17.79	11.36	22.19	933 (100.0)

Note: Figures in the table indicate row percentages.

a paucity of a systematic data base. The most readily available information source is the Housing and Population Tables from the decadal census operations. Even in these, however, there are problems of spatial compatibility. While the data for 1961 and 1971 refer to the AMC area, for 1981, the reference is to the Ahmedabad Urban Agglomeration. Estimates for housing stock in a given housing market first require a proper delineation of the local market itself. Table 3.7 is based on the delineation of the local housing market for Ahmedabad.

These estimates suggest that accretions to the housing stock, within the urban agglomeration area during 1971–81 decade, were at a faster pace than the earlier decade. A significant aspect of this growth trend is that within the municipal limit, there has been a deceleration in the housing activity. In the walled city, we even find an absolute decline in the residential housing stock. Thus, the major proportion of the accretions to the stock seems to have taken place in the eastern and western periphery.

Further, some proportion of the stock is also likely to remain vacant. There is an increase in the vacancy rate from 4.72 per cent in 1961 to 9.63 per cent in 1981. In a growing metropolis like Ahmedabad, the increase in vacancy rate in the light of the substantial demand for housing is surprising. Our estimates of vacancy rates within the fort walls of Ahmedabad are nearly 15 per cent. (This may partially explain the decline in stock of occupied residential housing.) These high vacancy rates do not seem to be related to residential mobility as the mobility rates observed are extremely low. Large proportion of housing remains vacant probably due to speculation. The present Rent Control Legislation may have a significant influence on rental market and as a result, the owners prefer to keep the houses vacant for prospective sale rather than rent (Table 3.6).

TABLE 3.6
Housing Stock in Ahmedabad

	1961 (AMC)	1971 (AMC)	1981 (AUA)
Total Census Houses	279640	337720	628380
Occupied Residential Units	222878	267620	480490
Vacant Units	11036	24775	51230
Other Uses	45726	45325	96660
Vacancy Rate*	4.72	8.47	9.63

* Vacancy rate is defined vacant units as a percentage potential residential stock. It is assumed that all vacant census houses are a part of the potential residential stock.
Source: Census of India, Vol. 5, Gujarat 1961, 1971, 1981 Reports on Housing Tables.

In order to understand the quality of the existing stock and its distribution across different groups and areas in the city, it is necessary to understand the heterogenous nature of the bundle of characteristics which generate a flow of services to the users. The most important of such attributes are the material quality of shelter, size, infrastructure services and location.

MATERIAL QUALITY OF SHELTER

One of the most useful variables in this regard is the house type which may be essentially a proxy variable for many characteristics. About 12 per cent of the stock consists of 'pol' housing found within the fort walls. The rest of the stock is almost equally divided amongst the poor quality of the huts and chawls on one hand and the other housing, either apartments or individual houses, representing better material and service quality on the other hand. The former is largely concentrated in the eastern areas whereas the latter is in the elite western areas.

TABLE 3.7
Estimation of Housing Stock for Local Housing Market

Zones of the City	Year		
	1961	*1971*	*1981*
Fort Walls	78517	80697	78257
East AMC	114110	163015	208974
West AMC	26079	49670	82689
AMC Total	218706	293382	369920
		(34.14)	(26.10)
East Periphery	15603	25923	77168
West Periphery	5604	10297	45541
Total	240813	339602	492629
		(41.02)	(45.06)
Estimated Total Housing Stock	252742	371028	545124

Source: General Population Tables, Census of India, 1961, 1971, 1981.
Notes: 1. Figures in parenthesis are decadal growth rates.
2. The local housing market includes a few additional areas besides those covered in the Ahmedabad Urban Agglomeration as defined in the Census of India.
3. The figures refer to occupied residential Units.
4. Total Housing stock is estimated by using the vacancy rates reported in Table 3.6.

The average age of a house in Ahmedabad is 34.7 years. We find that the housing stock in the walled city of Ahmedabad is on an average more than 60 years old, with almost one-fourth of the stock over 75 years old. The age of dwelling unit is usually associated with the structural condition and habitable quality of shelter. The pols and chawls have a large stock of older buildings whose structural conditions have been deteriorating, in absence of proper maintenance.

In terms of material quality, we find that only 8.4 per cent of the total stock consists of undurable (*kutcha*) roof and wall materials. Even amongst hutments, only 46 per cent have undurable roof and wall material. On the other hand, nearly one-fourth of the chawl and pol housing have undurable roof material. The building materials for the roof and walls in the chawl or pol housing is indicative of the poor maintenance in these units. A plausible explanation for this is the fact that the chawls, which were initially constructed as low cost rental housing units, are no longer a profitable enterprise for the owners as the rents have been pegged at the level of 1947 due to the Rent Control Act. Suitable fiscal and legal measures are required to ensure appropriate maintenance of these units.

Size of Dwelling

The other important characteristic is the size of the house. In Ahmedabad, 41 per cent of the housing stock has less than 25 sq.mts. of built-up area. With the average occupancy rate of 5.5 persons per dwelling unit, we find that, on an average, a resident in Ahmedabad has only about 4 sq.mts. of built-up space in the house. The built-up area of dwelling units by the spatial zones in the city indicate that within the Ahmedabad Municipal limits the dwelling areas are generally larger than the peripheral areas. This is because the dwelling stock in the city is older than the dwelling stock of the periphery. With the increasing land prices and construction material costs, it is natural to expect smaller dwelling units in recent years. The information on built-up area by house types indicates that while three-fourths of the huts and two-thirds of chawl housing in Ahmedabad, catering to the needs of the lower income groups, have a built-up area of 25 sq.mts. or less, even some of the 'modern' housing units like apartments, tenements and row houses also have almost one-fourth of the units below 25 sq.mts.

The exact nature of per capita space availability can be judged from its distribution amongst different income groups. Nearly 25 per cent of the households in Ahmedabad 'enjoy' a dwelling space of less than 2 sq.mts., a space which is just sufficient for an adult to sleep comfortably. This implies that one-fourth of the city population does not even have adequate sleeping place. At the other extreme, about 14 per cent of the households in the city enjoy per capita built-up space of 30 sq.mts. or more. The disparity in per capita built-up space is even more pronounced than the disparity in income levels. One of the major reasons for this to occur is the fact that the housing prices have probably increased at a more rapid rate than personal income and hence households which could afford to build or rent larger houses in the past, are now also compelled to be content with smaller dwelling space.

Infrastructure Services

A description of the housing stock in Ahmedabad would be incomplete without reference to the availability of basic services like water supply and sanitation facilities. While the civic authorities are required to provide these basic facilities, individual households have to pay for the installation and use of these services. In the peripheral areas, outside the limits of the Municipal Corporation, the village councils are required to provide these facilities. But we find that a large number of residents in the peripheral areas have to fend for themselves as the village councils are not in a position to meet these requirements.

Within the AMC area, at present, on an average, 190 litres per capita per day (lpcd) water is supplied. While this is in excess of the design norm of 140 lpcd used by the AMC itself, its distribution among the various zones of the city is uneven. Potable quality of water is supplied for purposes ranging from domestic use to gardening, with the result that residents in west AMC use as much as 250 lpcd of water as against only 50 lpcd available to the slum dwellers in East Ahmedabad.

Most of the water demand in peripheral areas is met by tubewells used to draw ground water. Industries in East Ahmedabad are also required to meet their own water demand. With intensive ground water withdrawals each year, the water table in Ahmedabad has depleted at the rate of 1.5 to 2.0 m. each year. It is thus becoming increasingly difficult to tap the ground water sources and at the present rate of withdrawal, the city is likely to face a severe water crisis in the next few years.

It may be presumed that households having water taps in the house are able to meet their daily water requirements, even if the supply of water is only for a few hours each day. We find that three-fourths of the households in Ahmedabad have at least one tap in the house. The condition in the eastern periphery is dismal as compared to the other zones as only 42 per cent of the houses have a water tap. Nearly two-thirds of the 'slums' housing in Ahmedabad do not have water supply at all. The chawls are a little better-off as only one-third of houses do not have their own water tap. Some of the row houses/tenements in the eastern periphery also do not have easy access to water.

While the water supply situation at the aggregate level indicated that nearly three-fourths of the population of Ahmedabad had individual access to drinking water, only half the population had its own toilet, and another 14 per cent of the households did not even have access to a public toilet. The situation with regard to sanitation facilities is fairly serious in the peripheral areas, particularly the eastern peripheral areas where nearly 40 per cent of the households are devoid of any access to even public toilets. On the whole, about one-third of the households depend on public or common toilets, the quality of which is often appalling—particularly in the slum areas, where only one toilet is provided for 30 households.

While the water supply and waste water collection systems are provided by the local authorities, it is likely that 'unrecognised' shelter stock may not be provided with these facilities by the local authority. The electric supply within the city is provided by the Ahmedabad Electric Company, a private utility firm which, at least in principle, provides domestic connection to all households which can pay for the installation costs. Despite this easy availability of electricity, we find that nearly 18 per cent of the houses in Ahmedabad do not have this facility. The situation is worse in eastern Ahmedabad where one-fourth of the households do not have electricity. A few enterprising households have managed to get an illegal electricity connection for which they do not pay any charges except occasional bribes to the officials of the company.

The situation is even worse amongst the slum dwellers where almost 73 per cent of the households do not have electricity. Nearly one-fourth of the chawl houses also do not enjoy electricity. However, in a majority of the slum and chawl settlements within AMC, street lights are provided by the Municipal Corporation, which provide some illumination to the otherwise dark neighbourhood. In the slum settlements in the peripheral areas, even this source of illumination is absent.

Land, Economy and Housing

From the diverse trends in the spatial patterns of population and housing and the changing economic structure of the city, some interesting insights may be developed into their probable interrelationships.

LAND

The rapid growth in housing stock in the peripheral areas of the city during the past decade is indicative of both greater availability of vacant land and relatively lower prices in these areas. In economic terms, the price of land is the present value of a discounted stream of earnings in the future. Agriculture, with its lower returns, is easily outbid by non-agricultural uses in the urban fringe areas, and in a dynamic perspective the city extends outwards each year.

Land prices in urban areas follow a distance-decay pattern, that is, prices decline with distance from the core of the city. Ahmedabad is no exception to this pattern, as we see on examination of data on registered land prices. It is also natural to expect that the distance-decay relationship is likely to be different for various sectors of the city. This is largely on account of spatial distinctiveness of uses in various sectors of the city. For example, the western sector of Ahmedabad has emerged as an upper class residential area, while most industrial establishments are concentrated in the eastern sector (Table 3.8).

The information used for the above analysis is deficient in the sense that it does not necessarily depict the market price which may be substantially higher. This happens as the registered price generally excludes the 'black money' component. However, cross-checking with the available data on actual market prices for similar localities suggests that this component has been significant only in the eighties (Wadhwa, 1987). Further, as there does not seem to be any distinct spatial bias in the difference, it is safe to assume that the spatial trend in price rise as suggested by our data is largely correct. In general, the rise in prices is far more pronounced for the peripheral areas as compared to the core city areas. This is similar to the trend observed in Latin American Cities (cf. Mohan, and Villamizar, 1980).

URBAN LAND CEILING

Land prices are influenced by the prevalent legislations. The Urban Land (Ceiling Control) Act of 1976 was promulgated with the main objective of 'preventing the concentration of urban land in the hands of a few persons'. The Act specified a ceiling limit of 1000 sq.mts. of vacant land in and around Ahmedabad city. The State Government could acquire land in excess of the prescribed ceiling by paying a meagre financial compensation.

TABLE 3.8
Land Prices in Selected Locations of Ahmedabad

Locations	Land Prices in Rupees per sq.m.				Percentage Growth Rate
	1961	*1970*	*1975*	*1980*	*1971–'81*
Fort Walls	145	363	469	560	54
West AMC					
Ashram Road	79	223	435	520	133
Kochrab-Paldi	34	150	179	239	59
Usmanpura	32	112	—	312	178
Vadaj	24	75	146	162	116
East AMC					
Asarwa	134	143	257	286	100
Maninagar	32	95	141	220	131
Khokhra-Mehmedabad	40	75	196	170	126
Rakhial	27	175	230	255	145
West Periphery					
Vastrapur	5	41	56	65	158
Memnagar	2	27	68	74	174
Thaltej	1	5	15	18	260
Vejalpur	3	11	39	56	409
East Periphery					
Naroda	7	26	68	95	265
Odhav	8	33	83	103	212

Source: Compiled from Records of the District Collectorate, Ahmedabad.
Note: The prices listed above are average registered sale price for each zone. The averages were computed from all the transactions carried out in the year.

It is more than a decade since the promulgation of this Act. However, a main purpose of the Act, in terms of land acquisition, has simply failed to materialise. The excess land acquired under this Act is just 0.3 per cent of the estimated surplus land. The remaining land has been either caught up in endless court litigations or held up under pending applications for exemptions under Section 21. On the other hand a large number of owner/developers have been exempted under different sections. For example, Section 20 of the Act provided exemption with respect to hardships to land-owners or cases involving public interest. Under Section 21 of the Act, the excess vacant land would be exempted from acquisition if housing for weaker sections was to be built.

Two major areas of impact of ULC are widely believed to be in a reduction in the supply of land and the resultant steep rise in land prices. Our analysis of the Ahmedabad experience suggests that both of these were probably only short-term impacts. Conceptually, it has been argued that due to the ceiling limits only smaller plots below the ceiling limits would be available in the market. This would then 'artificially' restrict the supply and with a continuing demand for land, this would result in a price rise (cf. Wadhwa, 1987 and NCU, 1987). In empirical terms, there is meagre evidence to indicate that such price rise has actually occurred.

The short-term impact of Urban Land Ceiling in Ahmedabad has been an increase in the supply of housing. Conceptually, in a micro-economic perspective, a landowner would put his land in the market if the difference between the present value of the perceived stream of net earnings in the future, is less than the perceived current market price. For an individual landowner, this would also be linked to his own holding capacity, so that a large owner with other assets would be able to hold the land off for a longer time. The effect of ULC, in the short run, was to drastically lower the landowners' perception regarding the future earnings. This increased the propensity to sell and/or develop the land for a large number of landowners. It is likely that this was facilitated by a base of well-developed builder groups in the city. A large number of exemptions were sought and granted in Ahmedabad under Sections 20 and 21 which were essentially handled by these builder firms. A review of building sanctions granted by AMC also shows an upsurge during the three years following the Act. This, however, was a short-run effect as the supply has since then stabilised.

The process was also facilitated by certain political factors. 1977 elections, following the national 'emergency' saw the emergence of a coalition of opposition parties at both the national and the state level. Given the diverse composition of this new political party, the landowners' and developers' lobby had little difficulty in claiming the necessary exemptions under the Act. This was done by extending the deadlines for application, including cooperatives and industrial workers' housing under the guidelines for Section 20, and later under Section 21. In fact, the number of dwelling units approved during the seven year period from 1977–84 under the ULC itself is much larger than the estimated formal sector supply based on past trends.

Despite this short-run increase in supply, it is doubtful whether there was any increase in housing for the economically weaker sections, neither through public housing on acquired land nor through the exemptions. Most of the houses built through these exemptions were for the middle and upper income groups. Since the Act has also prescribed the limits on the size and sale prices of houses built under Section 21, a large amount of transactions were carried out with 'black money'.

This sudden spurt in the supply for specific sections of consumers was not matched with any rising demand. In fact, both the speculative and consumptive demand have probably been restrained during the eighties. Thus, the Ahmedabad housing market now faces a reversal. During the eighties, the housing prices have not increased significantly in real terms.

On the whole, the Urban Land Ceiling Act despite its progressive ambitions towards a more equitable society, has not benefited the real low-income groups in the city. In the short-run, however, it did lead to a largely unintended effect of a spurt in the housing activity in the city, further aided by the transfer of finances from the Textile industry and a buoyant private sector developer group in the city. This provides an important lesson in the use of indirect measures to influence the land and housing market.

The second important component of housing costs besides land, is the cost of construction. As compared to the other metropolitan cities, the building cost index of Ahmedabad shows the least increase. This may be partly reflected in the high rate of building activity in Ahmedabad especially during the seventies (Table 3.9).

CITY ECONOMY

While the price of land and building material have a direct influence on the price of housing, the general economic conditions in the country and particularly in the city influence the level of activity in the housing sector. The construction sector itself contributes very little to the city's income. Kashyap, et al. (1984) estimate the construction industry's share as only 4.5 per cent of the total city income in 1976–77. The investments in the housing sector are, however influenced by the surplus generation within the city economy and investment of this surplus among competing sectors. Within a portfolio of investment possibilities, real estate is generally found to be more prominent. This is largely due to the higher rates of return offered by the sector as well as its ability to absorb and circulate the 'black' money.

TABLE 3.9
Building Cost Index Numbers of Government Construction for LIG Houses

Year	Cost Index (1970 = 100)		
	Ahmedabad	*Madras*	*Delhi*
1970	100	100	100
1972	108	88	272
1973	117	98	288
1974	155	115	332
1975	169	159	356
1976	169	167	388
1977	178	170	406
1979	224	245	510
1980	266	283	593
1981	271	317	670
1982	263	386	759

Source: National Building Organisation, *Handbook of Housing Statistics*, 1978–79, 1982–83.

The buoyancy of the city economy influences both the volume and nature of housing activity. In a growing economy with a highly skewed income distribution, it is evident that the benefits of the economic gains accrue to a very select group. Though this group may not have a significant consumptive demand for housing, it has a purely speculative motive in residential housing investment. The top three deciles of the income class also have a genuine consumptive demand for housing. These demands are met both by the housing producers as well as speculators. The consumptive demands for households below the medium income are primarily met by the informal or quasi-legal sector which has a large turn-over of stock, but has a lower value associated with its investments.

We do not have any time-series estimates of the city's income to relate to the level of housing activity. One can, however, take some clues from the pioneering study of Kashyap et al. (1984) which presents the city's income estimates for 1976–77. They found that of the total city income of Rs. 579 crores, nearly one-half was the contribution of directly productive activities. The predominance of the textile sector in the city is apparent from the fact that one-fourth of the city's income (Rs. 145 crores) was generated by the textile sector alone. In the same study, they also identified a strong inter-dependency of the other manufacturing and service activities to the textile sector. Ahmedabad's economy, is thus found to be greatly influ:nced by the level of the textile sector activity.

In terms of the factors influencing the housing investments in the city, it is almost impossible to generate reliable estimates from the readily available data sources. However, by collecting diverse information and a general awareness of the trends in the city economy, it is possible to put together a plausible scenario.

As we discussed earlier, the textile industry in Ahmedabad was probably at its peak in the early seventies. Although the actual mill closures started after 1979, it is most likely that the flight of capital from textiles started in the second half of seventies. This provided a boost to the upcoming housing industry in the city, which had begun in the early seventies but flourished during the latter half. Further, the entreprenurial ability of the local elites played a key role in such investments. At the same time, the speculative demand in housing was probably quite high. This was because the substantial rise in prices during the seventies ensured a high return from capital gains. On one hand then, these factors probably led to a high level of housing investment in the city, which was also backed by a consumption-based demand. The latter was probably steady as despite moderate population growth rates, incomes were high and access to institutional financing through the cooperative sector was ensured, especially for the upper and middle classes.

During the early eighties, however, the situation underwent rapid changes. While on one hand, the economic base of the city was severely affected, the increased housing activity of the seventies led to a glut in some of the sub-markets. This is, of course, compounded by at least two other factors: with the severe strains posed by the economy, household incomes have probably been adversely affected. As the distribution of household income is probably regressive, the income distribution has worsened considerably. The overall effect has been to depress the level of housing demand.

Simultaneously, the speculative demand must have also received setbacks due to the perceived problems in the city's economy and a lack of consumption-based demand. Perceptions further worsened with a spate of communal riots during the early eighties. The major source of institutional finance, through the cooperative sector is also not forthcoming. Although Housing Development

Finance Corporation has emerged as a significant alternative, its reach so far has been very limited.

Thus, the housing activity in Ahmedabad appears to be conditioned by the fortunes of the leading sector and consequently the economic health of the city. The schematic relationship presented in Fig. 3.1 is deduced from the descriptive analysis presented above. The jagged relationship is hypothesised as the investment decisions in housing are made on the basis of the surplus generated within the city economy.

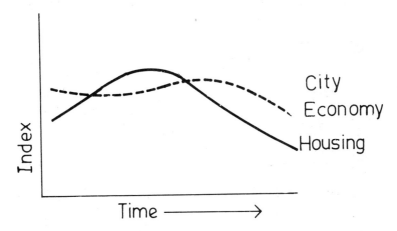

FIGURE 3.1 : City Economy and Housing Activity

On the whole then, it appears that the situation has probably reversed during the eighties. The formal housing activity, especially through the private developers, and the price rise during the eighties have slowed down considerably. Whether the benefits of slow price rise accrue to low income groups, will depend partly on the level of housing demand and the preferences amongst them. These issues are explored further in the following chapters.

TABLE A 3.1

Organised Sector Employment, Ahmedabad District, 1961, 1971, 1981

Code	Industrial Division	Percentage to Total Organised Sector Employment			Rate of Growth in Employment	
		1961	1971	1981	1961–71	1971–81
0 & 1	Primary Production	0.1	1.6	1.1	1424.0	–12.3
2 & 3	Manufacturing	70.5	57.5	57.3	10.8	24.5
4	Construction	4.0	3.6	2.8	22.3	– 2.1
5	Utilities	1.9	1.8	1.6	34.6	6.7
6	Trade and Commerce	2.1	6.3	8.4	308.6	67.7
7	Transport and Communication	4.3	5.9	6.0	85.1	27.2
8	Services	17.1	23.2	22.8	85.2	22.2
	Total Public Sector	25.2	34.0	38.9	83.3	42.9
	Total Private Sector	74.8	66.0	61.1	19.8	15.8
	Total Employment	100.0	100.0	100.0	—	—
	Total Employment in organised sectors	223,623	303,707	379,683	35.8	25.0
	All non-agricultural workers (census)	*477,557	599,600	838,443	25.5	40.2
	Organised Sector to total workers	46.8	50.6	45.3	—	—

Source: 1. Data organised sector employment from Employment Market Information.
2. Workers 1961, 1971, 1981. — Census of India, 1981. Series 5. Gujarat, General Economic Tables.

Notes: 1. For all workers (census), the Census Industrial Category I and II (Cultivators and Agricultural Labourers) are not included.
2. Workforce for 1961 is adjusted for definitional changes.

TABLE A3.2
Distribution of Income in Ahmedabad, 1984

Decile Group	Average Household Income (Rupees per month)	Share of Total Income (Per cent)
Lowest	290.43	1.76
Second	474.90	3.04
Third	664.97	4.26
Fourth	805.90	5.17
Fifth	974.35	6.25
Sixth	1184.45	7.61
Seventh	1475.90	9.47
Eighth	1873.02	11.89
Ninth	2669.86	17.14
Tenth	5081.00	32.99
Total	1560.80	100.00

Source: Primary survey.

TABLE A3.3
Stage in Life Cycle of Households

Zone of Residence	Life Cycle Stages					Total
	Young, Single/ Married, No Children	Young Married with Children Aged under 10 Years	Married with Children 10–20 Years	Married with Older Children	Old (55 yrs. and above) with Married Children	
Old City	17.60 (20.56)	19.20 (10.34)	29.60 (13.65)	30.40 (14.18)	3.20 (7.27)	135 (13.4)
East AMC	10.28 (43.93)	24.07 (47.41)	28.23 (47.60)	32.82 (55.97)	4.60 (38.18)	457 (48.98)
West AMC	12.67 (17.76)	20.67 (13.36)	32.67 (18.08)	26.00 (14.55)	8.00 (21.82)	150 (16.08)
East Periphery	18.84 (12.15)	38.10 (24.14)	24.49 (13.28)	19.73 (10.82)	8.84 (23.64)	147 (15.76)
West Periphery	11.11 (5.61)	20.37 (4.74)	37.04 (7.38)	22.22 (4.48)	9.26 (9.09)	54 (5.79)
Total	11.47 106	24.87 232	29.05 270	28.72 268	5.79 55	100.0 932

Note: Figures in the table represent row-wise percentages.
Figures in parenthesis are column percentages.

TABLE A3.4

Per Capita Built-up Area of Houses in Various Zones of the City

Zones	Per Capita Space in Sq. Mts.						Total
	Less than 2	3 to 6	7 to 10	11 to 20	21 to 30	30 or more	
Old City	24.00	27.20	12.80	14.40	10.40	11.20	125
East AMC	27.13	34.57	9.19	10.72	4.38	12.25	457
West AMC	13.33	12.69	10.00	19.33	12.00	31.33	150
East Periphery	35.37	33.33	16.32	6.80	4.08	3.40	147
West Periphery	9.43	22.64	16.98	20.76	7.55	22.64	54
Total	24.79	29.18	11.38	12.56	6.55	14.38	933

Source: Primary survey.

Note: Figures in the table represent row-wise percentages.

TABLE A3.5
Access to Water Supply Facility by Zones and House Types

Zone/ House Type	Taps in the Houses	Public Tap	Community Tap	Others	Total
Walled city	87.20	9.60	3.20	—	100(125)
East AMC	78.56	16.41	2.19	2.84	100(457)
West AMC	84.67	12.0	2.00	1.33	100(150)
East Periphery	42.18	49.66	4.76	3.40	100(147)
West Periphery	81.13	7.55	3.77	7.55	100(54)
Total	75.11	19.53	2.79	2.58	100(933)
Huts	34.96	53.39	3.39	8.47	100(119)
Chawls	65.73	27.02	6.45	0.81	100(248)
Pols	87.50	8.04	2.68	1.79	100(112)
Apartments/ Tenements	90.27	7.05	—	2.34	100(298)
Row House/ Bungalows	82.47	14.28	—	1.94	100(154)

Source: Primary survey.
Note: Figures in the table are row-wise percentages.

TABLE A3.6
Sanitation and Drainage Facility by Zones

Zone	No Drainage or Public Toilet	No Drainage but Common Toilet Available	Drainage with Common Toilet	Private Toilet	Total
Fortwalls	1.60	2.40	37.60	58.50	100.00(125)
East AMC	7.45	4.81	28.88	58.86	100.00(457)
West AMC	9.33	5.33	6.67	78.67	100.00(150)
East Periphery	40.81	32.65	14.96	11.56	100.00(147)
West Periphery	26.41	15.09	18.86	39.62	100.00(54)
Total	14.09	8.68	23.68	53.45	100.00(933)

Source: Primary survey.
Note: Figures in the table are row-wise percentages.

4. Structure of Housing Supply in Ahmedabad

During any given time period a wide variety of changes occur in the housing stock of a given urban area. These may range from the usually recognised new construction to changes occurring as a result of upgradation processes. Unlike for housing demand, the influence of macro determinants is more pervasive in the housing supply processes. These range from the nature of construction and developer industry, the buoyancy of the urban economy, housing finance policies to local policies affecting the supply of serviced land. The situation becomes even more complex as housing supply in urban areas of developing countries involves an interplay of a number of different actors and a series of interrelated activities. It is in the light of these viewpoints that an inquiry of structure and determinants of housing supply in Ahmedabad was carried out. The emphasis is largely on the nature of supply in the last two to three decades.

Housing System in Ahmedabad

To understand the housing system, it is first necessary to clarify the conceptual basis of inquiry. Following Turner (1976) and Baross and Martinez (1977), it is possible to break down the housing supply process in terms of an activity-actor matrix. It is then the 'social organisation within which they pursue their activities' which becomes relevant for identifying the major systems of housing production in Ahmedabad.

We can basically identify five major actor groups who are involved in different activities in the housing supply process. The first three of these, namely, the state or the public sector, the private commercial enterprise and the petty landlord, represent the producing sector. The public sector essentially refers to a number of different agencies which are engaged in the provision of housing through a variety of schemes and programmes. The private, commercial sector has gone through substantial changes in the recent past with a distinct tendency for some of it to turn to both illegal and quasi-legal processes. The extent of illegality and scale of operations differ substantially amongst different firms as does the quality of the housing product delivered to the market. The petty landlord group essentially refers to the individual owner or landlord who does not comprise a firm but uses a single house or a very small number of properties as an asset base to generate income. Although he may also follow profit-maximising behaviour, he is different from a private firm, in terms of the scale and nature of his operations.

Distinct from this group which produces housing for sale or renting, there are community groups or individual households who are both the producers and the ultimate users. The community group is characterised by a common concern to achieve benefits-use values for their members and this group operates on the basis of group concerns and priorities. This may comprise of formal registered organisations or simply informal associations of co-residents, based on social or occupational affinity. Similarly, the behaviour of the individual household is characterised by utility maximisation and dominated by use values rather than profits.

The major components, which are relevant in any process of housing supply, are land, shelter (labour and material), the utilities and services and the neighbourhood environment. With respect to each of these, the important activities are design and promotion, resource mobilisation, construction or execution and lastly, occupation and maintenance. Different major actor groups are engaged in these activities in differing degrees. The nature of operations also differ considerably, depending upon the motivation. The social production of housing in a given urban setting may be illustrated by relating these components and activities to 'the actors who play an active role in bringing them together in the production process'. A given system of production is thus a reflection of different actions in the sphere of the four main components of housing supply, by different actors using different methods for gaining access to relevant resources.

The conceptual basis of the actors and activities described above leads to different systems of production of housing. In the developing world, it is also important to distinguish the housing supply process by its commodity type and the ways or means adopted for its production. These distinctions could be made on the basis of the dualistic models of the urban economy (Lewis, (1958), Geertz, (1963), Santos, (1979), etc.). Thus, for analytical purposes, we have identified the dominant housing supply processes as formal sector housing and informal sector housing. Figure 4.1 suggests the dominant characterisations of these two sectors in accordance with the actor-activity approach.

FIGURE 4.1
Housing Systems in Ahmedabad

Activities	Actors				
	Public Agencies	Private Commercial Enterprises	Petty Land-lords	Community Groups	Individual Family
1. Design and Promotion	●	●	●+	+	+
2. Resource Mobilisation	●	●	+	+	●+
3. Construction Execution	●	●+		+●	●+
4. Occupation/ Maintenance	●			+●	+●

● Formal Sector Housing.   + Informal Sector Housing.

Following Johnstone (1985), we define formal housing as 'that which is constructed through established institutions and conventions and meets, indeed relies upon, the existence of legally based building and planning regulations and property laws'. The informal is referred to as housing which is developed through some form of illegal activities and does not conform to the statutory 'modern (often Western)' standards of construction. Recently, there are situations where even the conventional modern housing is often considered unauthorised because all the necessary permissions are not obtained. However, the available data base does not permit us to distinguish this type. Hence, even within the broad dual categorisation, there are likely to be overlaps suggesting some sort of continuity in the market.

Within the broad categorisation suggested above, further

distinctions may be made on the basis of the housing types prevalent in the local market. Within the formal sector, the first division may be made between housing provided by *public* and *private* sectors. As we shall see later, within these supposedly distinct categories there are clearly areas which overlap. For example, for most of the public housing, the actual execution is done by the private contractors, whereas for a large proportion of private housing, financing is utilised from the cooperative sector. The private sector housing is further sub-divided into two main groups: *traditional housing* and *modern housing*. Most of the traditional housing date back to the pre-independence period and consists of two major house types, namely, the pols and the chawls. The pols are traditional residential areas in the Walled City. Physically, these consist of a group of houses ranging from 100 to 500 in number, clustered around narrow, meandering streets. The density of houses are generally quite high. Most of this housing dates back to about 100 years. Chawls represent low income rental housing. Physically these are small, one to two room houses grouped around narrow streets with shared facilities. The modern housing spans over a large period, although the spurt in this type has taken place mostly in the post-independence period. This housing is largely based on the western principles and standards, developed either by the owner residents themselves, that is *self-built* or a private enterprise firm, locally referred to as *private developers*.

The major distinction within the informal sector may be made in terms of the methods used to gain access to land. Housing developed on illegally appropriated land, is termed squatters; whereas that developed on legally owned or rented land but without the necessary permissions from the local authorities is referred to as *quasi-legal*. These distinct systems may be distinguished on a set of characteristics. The basic difference, however, underlies the motivations and legality of tenure and development.

The most dominant of these systems in Ahmedabad have been the formal private sector and the informal sector. Despite, or probably because of the housing policy emphasis on the supply of packaged housing, the share of public sector in terms of provision of housing has remained quite poor—at a mere 10 per cent of the total stock by 1981. The share of static traditional sector has come down to about 30 per cent from a very high 60 per cent just two decades ago. Till 1971, both the informal and formal modern private sectors were the important modes in Ahmedabad. They had contributed to an extent of 37 and 43 per cent to the net decadal increases from 1961 to 1971. However, since 1971 the modern private sector has become even more important and has more than doubled its share from 1961 to 1981. The dominance of this mode is clearly evident from the fact that it has contributed at an increasing rate to the net decadal increase in the housing stock. The surprising aspect is that the private commercial sector seems to have outpaced even the informal sector in this process. In the 1971–81 decade, the private sector contributed almost 60 per cent to the net decadal increase compared to just 26 per cent by the informal sector. Our estimation method appears to have over estimated the informal sector housing as a recent study in the city enumerated 87,200 slum houses in Ahmedabad Urban areas. Thus the dominance of the private sector in the Ahmedabad housing market may be even more pronounced than that indicated through this analysis.

The spatial distribution of housing stock indicates that the influence of the modern private sector has been much more pervasive on the western side of the city. On the eastern side, the private sector has played a major role in the peripheral areas where it has been possible to get land. The rising share of this sector is reflected in the fact that its share even on the eastern periphery has increased from 28 to 44 per cent. On the whole, however, on the eastern side, the share of informal housing has been much greater. By 1981, nearly 35 per cent of the households resided in the slum settlements in East Ahmedabad.

In the last two decades 46 to 50 per cent of the net additions to the housing stock in East Ahmedabad were due to the proliferation of slum settlements. The continuing high growth of hutments in the eastern area clearly reflects the locational importance for low income residents, who are predominant in this area. The need to be in a close proximity to their workplace is not only for saving the transportation costs but is related to the spatial patterns in the labour market. Studies have shown that both opportunities for better employment and returns for similar work are affected by workers' residential location (Mehta, 1982a and Swamy, 1983).

We thus find that despite the intensified public sector housing efforts in the last decade, the private sector's role in the net accretions to the housing stock has increased from 43.4 per cent to

TABLE 4.1
Structure of Housing Supply in Ahmedabad Urban Area

	Formal				Informal	Total
	Public	Private		Modern		
		Traditional				
		Pols or Gamtals	Chawls			
1961						
Old City	0.2	90.9	6.9	0.0	2.0	78517 (100.0)
East AMC	11.5	0.0	45.3	20.4	22.8	114110 (100.0)
West AMC	2.0	0.0	9.2	62.4	26.4	26079 (100.0)
East Periphery	16.1	1.9	0.0	0.0	36.9	15603 (100.0)
West Periphery	0.0	83.5	0.0	0.0	16.5	6504 (100.0)
Total	14133 (5.9)	86349 (35.9)	59456 (24.7)	39479 (16.4)	41396 (17.1)	240813 (100.0)
1971						
Old City	0.7	89.6	6.7	0.0	3.0	80697 (100.0)
East AMC	14.7	0.0	31.7	23.7	29.9	163015 (100.0)
West AMC	4.7	0.0	4.8	65.1	25.4	49670 (100.0)
East Periphery	6.5	31.9	0.0	28.2	33.4	35923 (100.0)
West Periphery	0.0	71.?	0.0	13.2	15.6	10297 (100.0)
Total	29153 (8.6)	91085 (26.8)	59456 (17.5)	82406 (24.3)	77502 (22.8)	339602 (100.0)

Table 4.1 *contd.*

1981						
Old City	0.7	88.0	4.4	0.0	6.9	78257 (100.0)
East AMC	16.5	0.0	24.7	24.3	34.5	208974 (100.0)
West AMC	7.8	0.0	2.9	67.1	22.2	82689 (100.0)
East Periphery	7.3	20.6	0.0	44.7	27.4	775541 (100.0)
West Periphery	4.9	21.7	0.0	67.0	6.4	45541 (100.0)
Total	49427 (10.0)	94706 (19.2)	59456 (12.1)	171264 (34.8)	117776 (23.9)	492629 (100.0)

Notes and Sources:
1. The area coverage for these estimates is same as the Frontispiece.
2. The totals are from occupied residential Units reported in the relevant Census of India documents.
3. For housing typologies, the sources are:
   Pols   : Census of India
   Chawls : Bhatt and Chavda (1972)
   Public   : Estimated from records of different agencies
   Informal: AMC Slum Census (1976) and VSF Slum Survey (1984), School of Planning (1985)
4. The Cell values in above table represent the row percentages.

58.1 per cent during 1971–81. Contrary to the experiences of other cities, the role of slum housing in Ahmedabad has declined in the last decade, as evident from its lower share in the net additions to occupied housing stock. A detailed analysis of the supply processes of each sector is thus important to gain an insight into the factors affecting the output of each sector, the actors and the activities within each sector and the beneficiary groups.

The Role of Private Sector in Ahmedabad Housing

When viewed very comprehensively, the formal private sector may be said to cover most housing operations in the city. We may, however, divide the privately provided housing in two groups, the traditional type and the more modern housing which has mostly come up in the post-independence period. In the pre-independence period, the traditional housing consisted of two dominant house types; the 'pols' and 'chawls'. At least about 85 to 90 per cent of

TABLE 4.2
Spatial Patterns of Net Decadal Increases to Housing Stock

	Formal			Informal	Total
	Public	Private			
		Traditional (Pols and Gamtals)	Modern		
1961–71					
Old City	18.3	42.1	0.0	39.6	2180 (100.0)
East AMC	22.0	0.0	31.5	46.5	48905 (100.0)
West AMC	7.7	0.0	68.1	24.2	23591 (100.0)
East Periphery	10.0	9.4	49.8	30.8	20320 (100.0)
West Periphery	0.0	50.1	35.8	14.1	3793 (100.0)
Total	15.2	4.8	43.4	36.6	98789 (100.0)
1971–81					
Old City	—	—	—	—	−2540
East AMC	23.0	0.0	26.5	50.5	45959 (100.0)
West AMC	12.6	0.0	70.1	17.3	33019 (100.0)
East Periphery	8.8	10.0	59.1	22.1	41256 (100.0)
West Periphery	6.4	7.2	82.7	3.7	35244 (100.0)
Total	13.2	2.4	58.1	26.3	153027 (100.0)

Source: As in Table 4.1

the population resided in such houses at the time of independence. Although both these types also represent private sector supplies, they have not grown in the post-independence period. We have thus focused more on the other developments in the last three and a half decades only.

At the outset. it is also necessary to identify two basic distinctions in the role of private sector. Essentially, it refers to both the private commercial sector which operates on the principles of profit maximisation and the community/household based housing which emphasises utility maximisation. Our overall analysis clearly reflects a growing importance of the private commercial sector or the 'builder/developers' as locally known, at the expense of more genuine 'popular sector', with housing organised and/or built by the community or the users themselves. This trend will have implications for the existing stock also as the house increasingly becomes a commodity rather than only a consumption good. Following Conway (1982), it then becomes necessary to identify the impact of this commoditisation and the nature of factors which have promoted such changes.

PRE-INDEPENDENCE DEVELOPMENTS

The very beginning of private efforts can be traced to the elite movements outside the walled city and the low income rental housing developed on a large scale in the form of chawl housing. The chawls were developed by both the private entrepreneurs and institutions. Although these provided only a bare minimum of physical comforts at extremely high densities, it was at least a form of shelter within the accepted legal framework. It appears that by 1930, almost 90 per cent of the households on the eastern side of the river resided in this type of housing. However, since independence, this form of housing has totally stopped. One explanation for this has been in terms of the effect of Rent Control Act of 1947, following which the investment in such housing ceased to be profitable. It is, however, not very clear as to whether this Act really had any decisive influence on the development of chawls. An alternative explanation may be that the chawls were not really being developed as profitable investments by commercial enterprises but constructed by industrialists and given at low rents to the new migrant labour to entice them to work in the rapidly developing textile mills. This seems quite likely as most of the growth in the textile sector also took place during the twenties and thirties and stabilised thereafter. After this period, the pool of labour was adequate for the textile industry so that the incentive of low-cost rental housing was not really necessary anymore. In any case, the conditions in the chawls since then had worsened considerably, due to both overcrowding and complete neglect by the landlords who presumably found it uneconomical and irrelevant to invest in the maintenance and upkeep of these buildings.

On the other hand, the private sector's role in the provision of housing for the middle classes has increased tremendously over a period of time. The lead for this, in terms of the spatial patterns, has come mainly from the elite movements. New areas, mainly housing the elite, were developed in three directions, across the river on the western side, northwards in Shahibaug and southwards in Maninagar. These were low density developments which emulated the modern British town planning principles of low-density and garden suburbs. The 'elite' residential areas were further enhanced by the development of major educational and health institutions—in contrast to the highly polluting textile mills on the eastern side. Further, these areas were based on the garden-suburb concept with low densities, wide roads and large plots. The role of the elite as a vested interest was also clear from the fact that most of the area covered under the schemes for infrastructure provision was in the richer areas, even though the development was more intense and faster in the eastern working class areas.

The elite, of course, were generally able to finance their own housing, though richly supported by the local authority in creating an 'appropriate' overall environment in the new areas. A part of this consolidation process was through the financing of middle class to develop their housing in these areas. Largely, this support has come through the financing of housing cooperatives by the government. The first cooperative in Ahmedabad was started as early as 1924–25, when a group of persons came together to develop a land sub-division scheme with optimal provision for buildings. Liberal financing made available from the Registrar of Cooperative Societies ensured that none of the members of this first venture had to pay an amount larger than the rent they were paying for their crowded quarters in the city. This effort proved to be a pathsetter with over a hundred different cooperative societies coming up during the next two decades. Most of these were developed in the western elite areas. They were generally developed on a community basis with a group of persons from the same caste, geographical origins or occupational backgrounds coming together to form the cooperatives.

On the whole then, at the time of independence, almost 70 per cent of the households resided in areas outside the walled city in two distinctly segregated housing types. Even though the private sector as a whole was quite large, the share of modern private housing was very limited. This was generally limited to housing developed by the very rich on large estates or by the upper middle classes through the cooperatives. However, the proportion of the population housed by this type did not exceed 7 to 8 per cent of the total population outside the walled city.

HOUSING COOPERATIVES IN AHMEDABAD

The decades following independence have seen a phenomenal increase in the role of private modern housing in Ahmedabad. Surprisingly, however, even in this short span of 35 years, this has undergone substantial changes. The first two decades of this period essentially saw a widening of the cooperative network on a fairly large scale. By 1970, there were more than 1,400 cooperative societies with an estimated 55,000 members. Most of these were low-density and sub-plot type developments with either independent bungalows or detached tenement-type housing. In the initial years the plots were quite large, ranging generally from 500 to 1000 sq.m. This was reflective of both the low land prices and the town planning regulations which required very large minimum plot sizes. During the sixties, the average plot sizes showed a gradual decline, with the range shifting to about 300 to 600 sq.m. per plot. Similarly, compared to totally individual plots, there was a greater tendency to have tenement type housing, where independent individual units were spaced closely together on jointly held land. This was totally in tune with the rising land and construction prices.

Throughout these two decades, the private sector modern housing was based on genuine cooperative efforts where people came together to manage their resources in order to generate the housing product for direct utility maximisation. The financial assistance available from the Gujarat Housing Co-operative Society to each member was about 50 to 65 per cent of the total cost of development.

The benefits of these developments have accrued very clearly to the upper-middle income groups. This is partly reflected from the fact that most of the cooperative housing came up in upper income areas like Ellisbridge, Navrangpura, Shahibaug, and Maninagar. Detailed analysis by Bhatt and Chavda (n.d.) indicates that by 1965, 81.3 per cent of the societies applying for financial assistance were located in these areas. Similarly 82.3 per cent of the members receiving loans were from higher caste groups and almost none of them had a monthly household income of less than Rs. 1000 (at 1965 prices). A detailed look at the spatial patterns of cooperatives indicates that over the years there was a gradual shift to other localities. However, even this trend seems to have reversed itself in the last two decades. This is partly indicative of the changes taking place in the structure of private sector housing in Ahmedabad.

EMERGENCE OF CAPITALIST FIRMS

Thus, till the 1970s, private housing was based on community-based ventures, amply supported by financial assistance through the cooperative sector. During the seventies, however, a number of changes occurred in this supply process. Basically, there was an increasing commercialisation of the private sector, initially led by the technocrat 'developers' and later by 'organisers' who were essentially financiers, coming forth to finance this low-risk and high-return industry. There were many factors responsible for this major change in the organisation of private construction industry.

First of all, with the rising land prices, technological developments and the taste influences of migrants from Bombay following the formation of the Gujarat State in 1961, the high density, multi-storied apartment buildings were gradually becoming more common. These were also economically more viable than the earlier individual bungalows and tenements. On the other hand, the land prices were rising at a much faster rate than the real incomes, so that the demand for sub-plot type developments was going down, at least within the city limits. Although this demand did shift outwards to the periphery to a certain extent, related Vacant Land Legislation of 1972 effectively put a constraint on this type of housing development. This became almost totally non-viable following the Urban Land (Ceiling and Regulations) Act in 1976. In any case, these newer type of developments required relatively more organisational and technical know-how and hence the entry of technocrat developers.

This trend was further strengthened during the late seventies. Over time, with rapidly rising prices and the constant ceiling on cooperative financing, the price to loan ratios for acceptable middle-income housing rose to such levels as to make this financing meaningless for the middle class.* At the same time, during this period the procedures for getting the necessary permissions became increasingly difficult, especially after the enactment of the Urban Land (Ceiling and Regulations) Act. These various factors provided a ready climate for the commercialisation of private housing. This was further strengthened by other economic developments. With the stagnation in the textile sector, capitalists were looking for better investments. The structure of developer industry itself underwent changes by replacing the dominant role of the technocrats, architects or engineers, with that of the financers and legal experts.

The increasing importance of the private developer firm is reflected in the formation of the Housing and Estate Developers' Association in 1980. Although the Association boasts of a membership of 450 firms, Wadhwa (1987) points out that this may be an exaggerated figure. It is difficult to find out the exact number of firms operating in the market. It is likely that a substantial share of housing supplies is by the relatively large scale developers. Informal discussions put this figure at least 50 per cent. During the seventies, their contribution to total new supplies has in any case been substantial.

This rise in private sector's role is also reflected in the fact that the rate of ownership housing has more than doubled in Ahmedabad from 17.6 per cent owners in 1961 to 36 per cent in 1981. However, these benefits have accrued to specific groups, probably even at the cost of other more disadvantaged sections. As, for example, although the overall crowding in terms of persons per room increased from 1961 to 1971, the increase was totally absorbed by the one-room houses where it increased from 4.35 to 5.14. In the larger houses with two or more rooms, there was even a decline. Similarly, the benefits of ownership are distributed in a spatially skewed manner. Thus, compared to an average 36 per cent ownership in the city, the western elite areas had almost 58 per cent owners compared to only 28 per cent in the eastern areas.

Another significant trend taking place in recent years is that of unauthorised construction. Indirect estimates suggest that within the Ahmedabad Municipal Corporation limits during the 1971–81

---

* With a ceiling on loans to individual members of cooperative housing society of Rs. 25,000, the price to loan ratio for most middle income housing had become 5 to 6 in this period as against 2 or less in the late sixties or early seventies.

decade, almost 35,000 units or almost 50 per cent of the net additions were made without the requisite permissions. Of these, however, a larger proportion is, of course, by the informal sector which probably added about 30,000 units. However, almost 11 per cent of the supply by the formal private sector was also unauthorised in the sense that the necessary permissions were not taken. The incidence of such unauthorised construction was probably the same in the peripheral areas at about 50 to 60 per cent of net additions to the stock. However, the magnitude in the periphery is almost a staggering 40,000 units.

TABLE 4.3
Estimates of Unauthorised Construction during 1971–81

	AMC	Periphery
	(Number of Dwelling Units)	
1. Total additions to the stock during 1971–'81	76538	75489
2. Building use permissions given by authority	42000	36000*
3. Estimated unauthorised construction	34530	40489
4. Estimated share of Informal sector	29878	10400
5. Estimated Private sector unauthorised construction	4660	30089

* The data base for the peripheries is extremely poor. We had firm data only for building permissions issued by A.U.D.A. during 1980, 1981 and 1982. The estimate is based on two assumptions. The magnitude was marginally lower in the earlier part of the decade and that about 80 per cent of the permissions are actually utilised.

Source: Rows 1 and 4 — Table 4.2
   Row 2 — AMC (1976) and estimates for Periphery.

Informal Housing in Ahmedabad

As most of the formal housing efforts, especially since independence, have catered only to the middle classes and above, the only recourse left for the lower income groups has been to live in the 'hutments' commonly referred to as 'slum' housing. The lower costs of housing in these settlements match the preference of these groups to minimise their housing expenditure.

SPATIO TEMPORAL PATTERNS

Although in 1981, the proportion of population residing in such settlements was not very high, especially as compared to other Indian metropolises, the past patterns reveal some interesting changes. On the whole, the proportion of informal sector housing has risen from 17.2 per cent in 1961 to 22.8 in 1971 and almost 24 per cent in 1981. However, its share of the net additions to the stock has declined, in the last decade. A spatially disaggregated picture suggests that in the Eastern AMC area, almost 50 per cent of net additions are by this sector. Similarly, in the eastern peripheral areas, the informal sector continues to be important, though not dominant any more.

On the whole, the years between 1961–71 witnessed a rather explosive growth of informal housing which showed an average decadal growth of 88 per cent compared to the overall growth in housing stock of only about 40 per cent. The next decade, however, shows a considerable decline with the growth rate at only around 50 per cent.

Using the data from the Slum Census conducted by the AMC in 1976, clear tendencies of saturation and outward movement of this type of housing are evident. In 1976, there were about 1250 slum clusters as identified by the AMC. The development of these clusters over space, suggests that the initial growth of slum settlements was more concentrated in areas close to the old city in the northern zones. During the fifties and sixties, development of slum housing was more pronounced in the eastern zone. During the seventies, this growth momentum has probably shifted to the eastern periphery. More than 50 per cent of the clusters in these areas have come up during this decade. The pattern of development in the AMC and Eastern periphery suggests that the growth of slum settlement, moves out in rings as inner areas begin to saturate. However, the overall analysis for the entire agglomeration area suggests that the eastern AMC as a whole, witnessed a substantial addition of informal housing.

NATURE OF INFORMAL HOUSING

It is common on the part of urban planners and policy-makers to regard the entire slum formation or informal housing as being of a rather homogeneous type. However, the generally similar physical character of these areas compared to the middle income housing areas hides the realities of their evolution. There are distinct patterns in their evolution and, for a given cluster, these also change over time.

Drawing on a number of studies which have directly or indirectly looked at the processes of evolution of slum clusters or settlements, there are two distinct types which seem to be prevalent in Ahmedabad. These types are identified mainly on the basis of the mode of access to land. The *squatter* settlements are developed on illegally appropriated land whereas the *quasi-legal* settlements are on legally owned or rented land but developed without the necessary permissions from the authorities. Within each group, further distinctions are made on the basis of the dominant actor groups involved in initiating these settlements.

SQUATTER SETTLEMENTS

The distinctive feature of these settlements is that land is usually appropriated either by a community for their own use or by an opportunist 'slumlord'. The land on which squatting occurs may be vacant either due to its unsuitability for conventional development (like low lying areas, river beds, marshy lands) or because it is under acquisition in accordance with the zonal plans of the local authority. Similarly, publicly owned vacant land is a prime target for appropriation. Often, lands under long legal disputes or owned by 'absentee' landlords are also squatted upon by the slumlords.

These type of settlements are more likely to come up near places of work. However, at times of emergency, due to riots, floods or forceful evictions, any potential site will be taken over—even if the location is inconvenient. Development then proceeds rapidly as relatives and kith and kin flock in, once some security is possible. In any case, larger numbers also tend to ensure security of tenure due to the political vulnerability of the situation. Households at all levels of the economic ladder may be found here.

For shelter, the most common form of tenure is that of owner-occupant only. Though there are some tenants, this is less common. The material quality of shelter depends generally on the income levels of the households. Thus, a great variety of levels are observed. In most cases, however, the scope to expand the area of the house is not present except for the more dominant households who generally keep larger areas for themselves. The latest trend in the slumlord type of settlements is quite promising, as the residents tend to organise, once the knowledge of the completely illegal position of the slumlords is discovered. The local leaders in many cases have overthrown the stranglehold of the slumlord and stopped paying rent to him. Further, the implicit policy of the Municipal Corporation and their legal position presents no possibility of eviction. In accordance with the Corporation's policy to provide the minimum infrastructure of common water taps, water-closets and individual drainage connections, a large majority of the settlements have obtained these.

QUASI-LEGAL SETTLEMENTS

The second group of slum settlements consists of quasi-legal sub-divisions and tenements. These settlements are different from the squatter settlements as they are built with the explicit consent of the land owner. Three identifiable models exist within this group.

Community Based Sub-divisions

In this case, a community, either on the basis of social or occupational groupings, buys or leases out land from a landlord often with the help of a middleman. The requisite sub-divisions and allocations are carried out by the group leaders, who also determine the land rents to be paid by the members. Shelter is developed by individual households according to their access to building materials. The settlements are quasi-legal, only in the sense that no formal approval for the land sub-divisions or buildings is sought from the local authority. The materials used for shelter are also usually 'temporary' and no building permissions are sought. The overall size is properly laid out, with emphasis, however, on maximising the use of land—even at the cost of environmental conditions.

Landlord Based Sub-divisions

In the second model of this group, a similar type of development is initiated by the legal landlord himself. In most cases the landlord operates through a middleman who often turns into a slumlord. There are two main reasons for a landlord to go in for promoting such development. A lot of areas which have been now engulfed by the urban growth of Ahmedabad were considered distant outlying areas just three or four decades ago. In those days it was quite profitable to rent out plots of land to low income groups who would then construct their own shelters/huts. Thus, without making any investments, the landlords collected rent for the land which often exceeded its market value.

Also, the possibility of eviction at that time was not as explosive an issue as it is today. Especially, in some clusters, the developments occurred before the enactment of the Rent Control Act. Subsequently, however, it has not been possible to evict the tenants who have generally become aware of their rights. These sites have also been developed overtime without much consideration to an efficient design of the layout. In this situation, the subsequent developments have been either community-based with further additions taking place through kinship arrangements, or the initial occupants have become 'slumlords' with new additions being controlled by them. In this case, the rents are generally high and strictly enforced. Any improvement of the shelter is not readily permitted nor is the security of tenure for the tenants assured. The slumlords take all precautions to prevent any organisation of the tenants. In such cases, the response of the landlords may be to take legal action (which is rarely successful), seek an intermediate solution of 'buying off' these people or those with political connections may manage to have their land 'acquired' for a public purpose.*

A second reason for the landlord to promote this type of development arises when the land is put under acquisition or reservation for some purpose. As the value of land to the owner is frozen, it may be more profitable for him to promote development of subdivisions and distribute these through an intermediary on collection of deposits and monthly payment of rents. In a similar case where the plot was under the 'green belt' of the local authority, it was found that the landlord had collected much greater returns than the 'pegged market price' of land (Mehta, 1980).

Owner Developed Rental Units

A variant of the above model is the one in which the owner even undertakes construction of shelter. In these settlements, neither land sub-divisions nor shelter construction are approved by the local authority. However, since the shelter construction is

---

* In the first case, the high rates of return on both residential and commercial developments would ensure substantial profits, even after paying off the slum dwellers. In the second case, the landlords manage to get an alternative plot of land which is free from any problems.

undertaken by the land owner, there is a uniformity in the building material usage and the plots are well laid out with high densities. Rents vary from Rs. 80 to Rs. 100 for a 10 sq.mt. of shelter space. The enforcement is extremely strict with defaulters being evicted outright. The security of tenure is thus totally linked to the ability to pay. Further, the provision of services by the local authority ultimately benefits the owners who generally increase the rents in such areas (Boni, 1985). The location of such settlements is, as in the previous case, on the peripheral lands which are either under acquisition or zoned for the green belt.

Of the various processes described above, it appears that within the boundaries of the local authority, the more predominant form of supply is the quasi-legal. This is partially evident from the fact that almost 80 per cent of the 'slum' settlements are situated on privately owned plots. At the same time, however, there is an increasing trend in recent years to appropriate public land for this purpose, especially in the eastern periphery which has been very recently annexed by the Municipal Corporation. Our studies indicate that these slums are less likely to be community based and are largely developed by intermediary 'slum-lords'. The publicly owned land is most vulnerable to squatting as there is inadequate supervision. There is also 'public' knowledge (or at least knowledge among the interested persons) about the developmental programmes of the local agency for a particular site. The slum-lords are swift to organise squatting on such lands.

The majority of slum settlements, located upon privately held lands are not squatter settlements of the type described in this paper. Were this to be true, it would have been an apt manifestation of 'take over' of the means of reproduction by the proletariat. Instead, we find that a growing petty-capitalist class which has strong links to the local polity, participates in the informal housing market. Though the scale of operation, both in terms of numbers and finance, is small, the rate of 'surplus' generated is even higher than in the formal sector.

Housing Efforts of Public Sector Agencies

In comparison to the private sector, the role of public sector has been very limited in actual housing supplies in Ahmedabad. By 1981, a little less than 10 per cent of the stock was produced through the public sector efforts. Over the last two decades, its share in net additions to the stock has even gone down. The first half of the current decade, however, shows some increase. The public sector consists of a number of different agencies which have over the years participated in the housing provisions in the city. A number of these agencies are actually state level statutory authorities, whereas the others are governmental departments or local bodies. These agencies have mostly concentrated on supplying housing as a packaged product and have thus been involved in almost all the activities which constitute housing supply. Of the multitude of agencies operating within the Ahmedabad Urban Agglomeration Area, only the Gujarat Housing Board, Ahmedabad Municipal Corporation, the Gujarat Slum Clearance Board and State Government through its Building and Construction Department have contributed significantly to the housing supply. In terms of the process of public sector housing, these agencies dominate the entire process, leaving little scope for any participation by the users. However, the private commercial sector also participates in the construction process. Besides the regular packaged public housing projects, the other important contribution of the public sector is in terms of land development or the provision of macro-infrastructure like major roads, parks and utility mains. At present, these are provided by the Town Planning Scheme mechanism.

Over the last three decades, the nature of public housing efforts have undergone some changes, even though the basic thrust has remained more or less the same. In terms of the sheer magnitude of exercise, the public sector effort has been considerable. The different agencies together have built over 66,000 units at an average rate of around 2000 units per annum. The pace seems to have quickened considerably in the eighties. However, this is partly due to a number of sites and services projects coming up in the last four years. As a matter of fact, in the eighties, 25 per cent of the 'units' are in the form of serviced plots.

In terms of the contribution by different agencies, the largest has been the Gujarat Housing Board (GHB). GHB, the oldest housing organisation in the State was constituted as a statutory body in 1960. A large share of its resources have flowed into Ahmedabad urban area. It is, however, likely that given the demands from other fast growing urban areas in the State, Ahmedabad will receive lower shares in the future. Besides GHB, which has contributed over 55 per cent to the public sector efforts, Ahmedabad Municipal Corporation (AMC), Gujarat Slum Clearance Board (GSCB) and the different State Government (SG) departments have been the other contributors. In the recent years, AMC has moved away from direct provision of housing. On the other hand, GSCB though formed as early as 1974, also as a statutory body under the Gujarat Slum Areas Act, 1973, has done substantial work only recently. In the last five years it has provided a phenomenal 4,400 housing units and another 2,800 serviced plots for the low-income groups. The State Government has of course largely concentrated on the provision of staff quarters for its own employees, with about 90 per cent of these for the low-income sections.

Gujarat Housing Board (GHB)

The early efforts of the GHB were largely confined to the provision of housing under the Subsidised Industrial Housing Scheme (SIHS). Almost all the projects under SIHS were concentrated in the industrial belt. Although initially given as rental units under the scheme, over the years most of the units were converted to owner-ship through a hire-purchase system. Since the seventies, GHB has initiated different schemes based largely on target groups defined on the basis of income. Although the initial emphasis was on the Economically Weaker Sections (EWS) and Low Income Housing (LIG), the emphasis is now shifting towards Middle Income Groups (MIG). This is partly reflective of the problem of rising costs and the failure to revise the norms for income, housing standards or cost ceilings by the funding agencies. On the whole, however, it appears that despite its obvious success in terms of sheer magnitude, where it compares favourably on the national scene also, GHB has not been very innovative as regards the nature of schemes undertaken. Except for an isolated showpiece project of sites and services, it has totally shied away from any efforts at land development, even though this is permissible under its statutes. Even in spatial terms, GHB's emphasis is shifting towards the western higher income areas compared to the early siting for the majority of projects on the eastern side. A review of the on-going and proposed projects shows that almost 77 per cent of the on-going projects and 94 per cent of the proposed projects are on the western side of the river. Similarly, almost 80 per cent of these projects are for the MIG and HIG schemes. On the whole, GHB's efforts appear to be concentrated simply on increasing

FIGURE 4.2 : Organisation of Housing and Urban Development Related Agencies

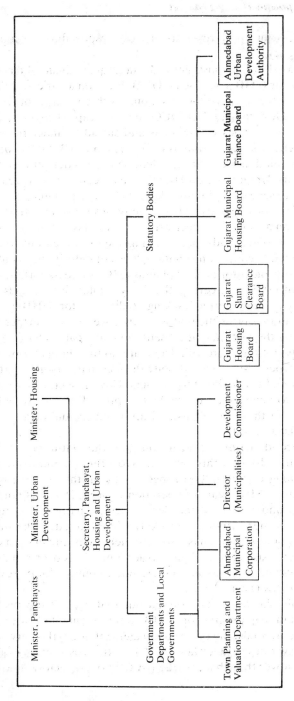

Note: The agencies in boxes are the ones which have had a significant role in the housing supply in Ahmedabad Urban Agglomeration Area.

the stock, without reference to its social responsibility as a public sector agency.

The second major constraint is the inadequate financial planning, especially for GHB and GSCB. GHB draws on a variety of different sources for resource mobilisation. Its three major sources are the State Government, HUDCO and the capital market. State Government, besides giving loans and subsidies under the social housing schemes, also channels LIG funds to GHB. GHB borrows from the capital market through floating its own debentures. Over the years its dependence on HUDCO also seems to be increasing.

There are several problems related to finance planning by GHB. A part of the problem arises from conditions for which GHB as an organisation may not be directly responsible. It is generally difficult for GHB to go in for advance planning due to two reasons. On one hand, the land acquisition situation does not indicate the availability of specific plots for project planning. But more important is the inability of GHB to ascertain the likely availability of funds even for a 3 to 5 year period making it difficult for GHB to plan activities and monitor them at a steady pace. This is further compounded by the fact that 'at present too many papers have to flow to government for approval'. There are no time limits for processing such papers. Moreover, despite the fact that very little outright subsidy or grant is provided by the State Government, it is necessary for GHB to have its annual budget 'approved' by the State Government. All these problems add up to substantial delays in the process (Isaacs, n.d.).

The second major problem concerns the statutory limits on resource mobilisation through State Government and debentures where ceiling of ten million rupees exists on the net borrowing. This curtails GHB's scale of operation. Since GHB does not have a sinking fund to refund the debentures at maturity, additional funds for further activities are likely to be limited in the future. GHB's accounting system is also extremely weak and in most cases full project costs are not taken into account. Costs over-run due to time delays and price escalations are not accounted for by revising the sale prices (Isaacs, n.d.).

It should, however, be pointed out that even if the resource mobilisation capabilities of GHB were augmented with pre-planning potentials, the project management in GHB is very weak. Despite low rates paid for land, GHB's actual costs for housing are not much lower than that provided by the private sector. A number of factors are responsible for this situation. GHB takes on far too many projects relative to its organisational capacity and its scheduled costs and completion periods are never achieved as it rarely undertakes pre-project planning.

TABLE 4.4
Gujarat Housing Board – On-going and Proposed Projects
(Number of Units)

	Spatial Pattern		Type of Scheme		Total
	East	West	EWS and LIG	MIG and HIG	
On-going Projects	2088	6856	4684	4260	8944
	(23.3)	(76.7)	(52.4)	(47.6)	(100.0)
Planned New Projects	9576	13836	3044	11668	14712
	(6.0)	(94.0)	(20.0)	(79.3)	(100.0)

Source: Gujarat Housing Board.

TABLE 4.5
Role of Different Agencies in Public Sector Housing Supply
(Percentage Distribution of Public Housing by Agency)

Year	GHB	GSCB	AMC	AUDA	State Govt.	Total
Till	63.9	—	10.2	—	25.9	100.0
1961	(29.4)		(11.1)		(47.5)	(21.4)
						14133
1961–'71	46.4	—	35.6	—	18.0	100.0
	(19.0)		(41.3)		(35.2)	(22.7)
						15020
1971–'81	68.2	1.2	24.0	—	6.6	100.0
	(37.8)	(3.3)	(37.6)		(17.3)	(30.7)
						20274
1981–'84	40.5	42.9	7.8	8.8	—	100.0
	(18.3)	(96.7)	(10.0)	(100.0)		(25.2)
						16648
Total	55.4	11.2	19.6	2.2	11.6	100.0
	36575	7400	12956	1461	7683	66075

Source: Compiled from Agency Records.

Similar problems confound GSCB, especially as it had expanded its activities rapidly in recent years. A major additional problem facing GSCB is the recovery of dues. The collection performance has deteriorated considerably with the arrears collection falling to 44 per cent in 1981–82 from 73 per cent in 1970–80. This is likely to become even more serious given GSCB's target groups. Besides low affordability levels, there is often political support and demonstration effect of earlier programmes which encourages the beneficiaries to default on repayments.

AHMEDABAD MUNICIPAL CORPORATION (AMC)

In comparison to GHB, AMC has attempted to change its approach to housing over the years. Although housing is only a discretionary function for AMC, in the early post-independence period it was engaged in the provision of packaged housing through different schemes. AMC's thrust has generally been on catering to the needs of the relatively low-income groups. The initial emphasis was on building new houses for the slum-dwellers under the Slum Clearance Scheme. In fact, AMC has built almost 10,000 units, referred to ironically as slum quarters. These are rental units, given at highly subsidised rents, and owned and maintained by the AMC. Despite regulations to the contrary, a large scale turnover has occurred in these, with the rental status being 'sold' at high premiums. Along with these efforts, the Corporation had also embarked upon other slum related schemes like Housing Accommodation and Slum Redevelopment which were mainly oriented to housing improvements at the same site. However, these have largely been aborted due to lengthy legal tangles over land acquisition.

AMC realising the non-viability of such schemes and their irrelevance to the total housing efforts required, has now turned its attention more towards environmental improvement programmes during the last decade. This is of course in keeping with the national level changes in housing priorities also (Mehta, 1986). AMC's switch over to improvement from relocation and public housing projects coincides with the central and state scheme of Environmental Improvement under the Minimum Needs Programme. However, the commendable action on AMC's part is that it has continued its efforts in this sphere despite its inability to avail of the 100 per cent financing available under this scheme due to contextual problems. In Ahmedabad, a large proportion of the 'slum' settlements are on private land or on reserved public land and hence the necessary guarantees could not be given by the local authority.* As a matter of fact, out of a proposed expenditure of Rs. 1.51 crores for provision of facilities on 393 different sites made in 1972 by AMC, only 37 were sanctioned at an expenditure of Rs. 1.7 million. Despite repeated requests by AMC, the stipulated conditions were not waived. AMC has, therefore, made legislative provision to give the necessary minimum infrastructure in both the slums and chawls, out of its own resources under the Environmental Improvement Scheme (EIS). It has spent almost two crore rupees in the last six years. Surprisingly, even here, the actual expenditure has generally lagged behind the planned expenditure. Further, the expenditure has slowed down considerably in recent years.

Besides the shared public facilities like water supply and toilets and individual drainage facilities given under the EIS, AMC also provides a high level of subsidy for giving individual water connections and toilets to the slum-dwellers. Although AMC has so far not paid any emphasis to giving tenure rights on a legal basis, security has been arranged through its 1976 Census of Slums when identity cards were given to each slum household. More recently, AMC also sought World Bank financing for an ambitious Slum Upgradation Programme which hopes to give legal tenure to almost all households in slum settlements. The major innovative aspect in this project relates to the use of the Town Planning Scheme mechanism for land acquisition. AMC thus hopes to circumvent the legal and financial tangles associated with attempts to acquire land under the antiquated Land Acquisition Act of 1894. A more direct element of cost recovery is also inbuilt in this process as generally required for any World Bank project (AMC, 1985).

In comparison to the more innovative AMC, the other public sector agencies have been rather lacklustre in their activities. GSCB has been a rather recent entrant in this sphere. Further, despite the statutory provisions, GSCB has not gone in for any

* The conditions required to be guaranteed for financial assistance are:
 i) The land-owner will not evict the inhabitants for at least 10 years,
 ii) No extra rent will be charged because of the improvements; and
iii) The landowner will not ask for more compensation because of the improvements.

improvement activities and has instead focused its approach entirely on public housing and sites and service type projects. In any case, its scale of operation has so far been quite limited. It is only in the last two to three years that it has expanded its activities considerably.

IMPACT OF PUBLIC HOUSING EFFORTS

It is clear from the above analysis that given the nature of efforts, public housing has had relatively little impact on the housing situation. Even in terms of the professed objectives of most schemes to reach specific target groups, the success can probably at best be termed as partial. There are two specific problems attached to this basic approach of public housing. Firstly the small number of highly subsidised projects leads to a tremendous competition. Thus it is probable that upward leakages take place in most of these projects. The pricing policy of most projects is highly subsidy-oriented, in order to be within the 'affordability' criterion. It is thus likely that the greater share of these subsidies accrues to the relatively better-off amongst the target groups. We have already seen indications of the changing emphasis of GHB in its recent investments. Both these processes together completely negate the whole basis of public housing approach as it is turned into 'a case of subsidising the rich' (Paul, 1972).

Besides the direct leakages, even the implicit subsidisation from different projects appears to be quite regressive. An earlier analysis by Paul (1972) of both the rental and hire purchase schemes by GHB suggests that the 'subsidies and windfall gains are larger for the more well-to-do among the income groups for whose benefit our housing schemes have been designed'.

Specifically his findings indicated the following imbalances:

— Within the low-income group rental housing schemes, rates of subsidy are higher for the larger and more costly tenements,
— The government's effective rate of return on low-income housing (hire purchase) seems to be somewhat larger than that on middle income housing, and
— The gap between the government's return and the private return . . . is very large and bestows substantial windfall gains on the middle income groups. Such gains are much less substantial for the lower income groups.

Even though Paul's findings were for schemes executed during the sixties, the pattern has remained the same over the years. Given the possible leakages, subsidisation and insignificant magnitude of public sector effort, there is an emerging emphasis on sites and services and slum improvement projects. Despite the 'universal' acceptance of this approach largely based on the World Bank's promotional efforts for their 'progressive development' model, the sites and services projects in Ahmedabad appear to have failed in many respects. First, the agencies have found it difficult to sell the serviced plots in comparison to packaged housing units. Second, even when they have managed to sell the plots, these appear to be much more in terms of speculative investments in land, since a large proportion of the plots (100 per cent in one of the first projects by GSCB) have been lying vacant while the other regular housing is, by and large, occupied. Third, even when the plots have been actually built upon, the construction quality clearly reveals leakages to higher income groups. In addition to these problems in implementation, the approach of the project design, has also been very imbalanced. The designs have been extremely inefficient leading to wasteful use of land and sub-optimal densities. This has been brought out in several studies which have analysed the site planning in many public housing projects (Reddy, 1984 and Sinha, 1982). Sinha illustrated that the total cost (of land and infrastructure) could be reduced by almost 30 per cent with better site planning without any loss in other qualitative parameters.

The reasons for these designs partly lie in the unfavourable location of these projects and their pricing policy. However, a more fundamental questioning in terms of the assumption of effective demand for legality from the lower-income groups on the one hand and the nature of supply processes need to be addressed to. Our studies of low-income supplies indicates that the popular sector, the main basis of progressive development approach, has become a total myth in Ahmedabad. Essentially, the sites and services approach represents a total commoditisation of land. When the total local market, both through its formal and informal sectors, has already been engaged in such a process, it is likely that a late entry by the public sector will succeed only if it gives distinct price advantages. Secondly, the locational priorities of lower income groups require better siting of projects which, can be difficult without an overall land policy.

Compared to the piecemeal sites and services projects by different agencies, the slum improvement programme by AMC has been, despite constraints, a much more comprehensive effort. AMC claims to have provided shared services to almost 90 per cent of the slum settlements. However, a recent evaluation by Boni (1985), reveals serious service gaps in its implementation. First, the services provided are generally inadequate in magnitude and often very badly located. The resultant pressure on the services and poor quality in provision often leads to poor maintenance and subsequent breakdown. This is especially true for the shared public services. The attractive subsidies for individual facilities are often not availed of due to tenure problems since the owners' sanction is essential. In other cases, it was found that these subsidies are used by quasi-legal developers to provide public services. These developers then charged extra rent for these better serviced units

Besides the problems in provision, AMC's main drawback has been a lack of coordination between different departments giving services and those in charge of maintenance of these services. Thus, despite good intentions, the programme has often benefited the middlemen.

CONSTRAINTS IN THE PROCESS OF PUBLIC SECTOR HOUSING

Thus the public housing efforts, both in terms of its nature and impact has not been very successful but it would be worthwhile to identify the basic constraints which impede this process itself. The most basic problem probably relates to a total lack of an overall planning perspective which views the overall urban housing needs, as disaggregated by at least location and income. The role of the public sector should be viewed in this holistic perspective. As against this, almost all agencies adopt ad hoc measures, designed more to suit the requirements of the financing agencies and land availability. A review of agencies' planning efforts clearly reflect this ad-hocism.

AMC in its development plan envisaged an ambitious shelter programme. Similarly there were some efforts by AUDA aimed at evolving an overall urban housing strategy. However, both these exercises have made naive assumptions about housing demand patterns likely to prevail in the future. Similarly, there is no attempt made to evolve a clear understanding of the supply processes prevailing in the urban area. These attempts suffer from both methodological problems and extremely unrealistic assumptions of the role of public sector agencies. The projections are at best too simplistic and do not take into account standard procedures like trends in vacancy rates, occupancy rates and replacement requirements. Further considerations like demand and supply analysis are not even mentioned. The more problematic areas are the totally unrealistic assumptions regarding the public sectors' capabilities with respect to actual building and resource mobilisation. In both the strategy planning attempts by AMC and AUDA, the actual achievements are far below than those envisaged. These ambitious programmes do not even mention any change in the present institutional structure which could lead to the achievement of the targets.

Besides this lack of an overall planning perspective, the other constraints relate to the undue emphasis on packaged housing by most agencies and organisational constraints related to land acquisition and financial planning. One of the major problems facing even the public sector agencies is the availability of land for public housing projects at the right location and at the right time. These, of course, partly relate to an inadequate use of the land readjustment mechanism available to the city planners. The problem is, of course, compounded by the freezing of a large area of land under acquisition procedures due to the Urban Land (Ceiling and Regulation) Act. It is estimated that in Ahmedabad, nearly 80 hectares of land which was to be taken over by the public agencies, has been affected by this.

Summary

Despite a long history spanning over five centuries, the most important developments in the residential structure of Ahmedabad have occured only in this century. Even within this, the most dramatic changes have taken place in the last two to three decades. A review of housing supplies in Ahmedabad indicates certain distinct systems in both the formal and informal sectors. Important amongst these are the public housing, traditional private sector, community based formal sector and modern housing which is commercially provided by the private firms. Within the informal sector also, clear distinctions exist in terms of community based housing and that produced by the petty-capitalists. In both the formal and informal sectors, there has been a gradual shift from traditional self-built housing in the early twentieth century towards commoditisation by the petty capitalists in the informal sector and the large housing firms in the formal sector. The importance of popular participation in the housing supplies is thus slowly being undermined. For the two important housing supply systems, the private sector and the informal sector, the more dominant role of the user groups has gradually been replaced by the capitalists as indicated in Figure 4.3.

The process of commercialisation of housing may either result from internal factors related to the users in terms of changing household situations or due to a set of external factors more related to overall conditions in the housing market in terms of nature of demand, levels of supply, flow of finance, profitability and prices and complexities involved in housing supply. On the whole, in Ahmedabad the latter have been greatly influential.

Firstly the conditions in the urban economy, in terms of the relative stagnation and closure of many textile mills has had a two-fold influence. The lack of employment opportunities in the textile mills has probably forced a large number of households, especially in the eastern belt, to turn to petty landlordism (cf. Mehta and Mehta, 1987). More importantly, through a rising demand, inflow of external capital for speculative activities (largely from Bombay) and unintended effects of certain legislative measures (especially ULCRA), led to the entry of private firms into the housing market in a big way.

In the informal sector, the 'slum-lordism' and quasi-legal developments are increasingly becoming commonplace. This process of commoditisation is probably not only restricted to the flow of new housing but also affects existing stock, especially in areas which lack effective and representative community control. Thus, the highly celebrated popular sector of the sixties is fast becoming a myth in both the formal and informal sectors with the rising domination of the capitalist form of production, both through small petty contractors/slumlords and individual households becoming landlords.

The effects of this pattern of development is mainly in terms of the loss of popular control over housing for a large proportion of the population. In effect, there is a gradual commoditisation of the housing product. The use-values are undermined by the actual or

FIGURE 4.3
Changing Structure of Housing Supplies
PRIVATE SECTOR

Activities	Actors				
	Public Agencies	*Private Commercial Enterprises*	*Petty Contractors and Land-lords*	*Community*	*Individual Family*
1. Design and Promotion		+		●	●
2. Resource Mobilisation	●+	+			+●
3. Construction/ Execution		●+	+	●	●
4. Occupation/ Maintenance				●+	●+

Activities	INFORMAL SECTOR				
			Actors		
	Public Agencies	*Private Commercial Enterprises*	*Petty Contractors and Land-lords*	*Community*	*Individual Family*
1 Design and Promotion			+	●	●
2. Resource Mobilisation			+		●
3. Construction/ Execution			+	●	●
4. Occupation/ Maintenance	+			●	+●

Note: ● Early Pre-1960 developments.
+ Post-1970 developments.

potential exchange or market value. This will not necessarily have adverse effects if the market is working efficiently and the supply-demand situation in different sub-markets is relatively balanced. However if house prices in real terms rise faster than actual incomes, the effective choice in the market will be reduced further and further. A greater tendency for forced immobility will then tend to characterise the housing process especially of the lower income groups.

While these trends characterise the private and informal housing supplies, the role of public sector has been extremely limited. In terms of direct provision it has had only a marginal effect. More importantly, there does not seem to be any marked change in the policy perspective. Clearly, the public sector's role needs to be transformed from direct provision to that of influencing the patterns of supply and housing market within a support policy framework.

5. Demand for Housing in Ahmedabad

Housing as an economic good is traded in the market like any other commodity. However, it has a number of distinct features that render the conventional demand theories inappropriate. Housing is today well recognised as a heterogeneous commodity which yields different services to different groups of people. It is, in fact, a bundle of diverse attributes and services, namely, space, physical quality, amenities, infrastructure, neighbourhood quality and location.

Location, or access to workplace, has been a distinctive feature of housing demand studies. An earlier recognition of this aspect lay in the observation that housing and employment accessibility are jointly purchased. Alonso (1964) examined the bid-rent curves within such a framework and identified the trade-offs between housing consumption and cost of transportation to work. The equilibrium condition in this framework was such that the marginal utilities derived by consuming an additional amount of housing was equal to the disutility of transportation cost. The trade-offs made by households between location and transportation (and other attributes of housing) are particularly relevant for the design of housing projects.

One of the shortcomings of Alonso's approach is that it ignores the durable nature of housing. The durability aspect relates to housing as both a consumption good and as an investment good. While housing decisions of tenants can be modelled as consumptive decisions, the owner-occupied housing represents an investment as well as the current consumption and, therefore, depends not only on contemporaneous variables but also on future expectations of capital gains. The housing investment, then, could be modelled by establishing a link between 'permanent income' and housing outcomes.

A local housing market operates within a set of regulations and controls established by the local and central authorities. Non-conformance to these regulatory measures has become a rule rather than an exception in most cities of the developing world. This has resulted in a variety of property rights and tenure relationships for housing. The prevalence of Rent Control Legislation has often led to 'pugdi' or key money payments for transfer of tenancy. The security of tenure attached to renting, squatting or owning a house is also an important determinant of a household's willingness to pay for housing.

Another aspect of housing which demands analysis is the difficulty of a majority of households to adjust their housing consumption in response to disequilibrium. Many households may prefer to remain in sub-optimal living arrangements rather than incur the costs of moving or modifying their existing structures. The estimated cost is not just the price of a new house or the cost of improvement but may also include information collection cost or emotional costs of leaving a place or modifying living arrangements. Since these costs vary across households, one may find similar households consuming different housing as well as similar housing with differing values or rents.

For an empirical analysis it is also necessary to bear in mind that measurement of 'quality' and 'price' of housing is difficult to assess. As discussed above, housing is a multifaceted good and the price of a house is not necessarily that of the shelter alone, but is also related to other attributes. The price of house must also take into account the key money of renters or unofficial (black money) payments of owners, the subsidies available with regard to housing finance and the distortions caused due to rent control measures.

Estimation of Demand for Housing Characteristics

Households with similar incomes spend differing amounts on housing. The numerous factors that determine households' demand for housing relate to their preferences for physical and locational characteristics of housing services. This estimation can lead to a significant understanding of the dynamics in the housing market.

Theoretical Basis of Estimation

The theoretical basis for most of the literature dealing with housing demand are pioneering studies by Lancaster (1966) and Rosen (1974) related to a single commodity with many characteristics.

Let $z = (z_i....z_n)$ be a vector of housing characteristics and $P(Z)$ be a hedonic price function defined by some market clearing conditions. The household decision is characterised by the utility function $U = U(X, Z)$, where X is a composite commodity other than housing whose price is unity. Households maximise utility subject to budget constraint $Y = P(Z_i) + X$. First order conditions yield, $P_i = \dfrac{U(Z_i)}{U(X)}$ or the implicit prices that households have assigned to the characteristics i.

Estimation of these implicit prices can be done simply by regressing the market values of the house prices P, as a function of various housing attributes.

Thus,

$$P(Z) = f(Z_i \ldots \ldots Z_n).$$

While the exact functional form of this equation is debatable, attempts have been made to estimate Box-Cox model which searches over alternative functional forms such as:

$$(P - 1)/\lambda = Bo + \sum_{j=1}^{m} {}_i B_j z_i, \text{ for } \lambda \neq 1.$$

Follain and Jimenez (1983), however, note that the functional form parameter, *lamda*, is consistently close to zero in most of the analyses in developing countries. This suggests that the semi-log specification is a good approximation to the best fit functional form. The analysis that follows is based on a log-linear specification.

The coefficients of the hedonic regressions are sufficient to reveal the preference structure. The marginal willingness to pay for a particular characteristic can be interpreted as the derivative of the hedonic regression with respect to that characteristic. Quigley (1979), however, asserts that this is not really true. The hedonic regression represents an estimate of the upper envelope of the bid-rent functions of different households for particular housing components. For any housing attribute, each bid-rent function is defined as locus of unit payments and amounts of that attribute yielding equal utility, with consumption of other housing attributes held constant. The same analysis can also be said to represent the lower envelope of the offer function of different suppliers for distinct housing characteristics. Thus the hedonic function represents valuation that is the result of demand and supply interactions of the entire market.

Within this perspective, the interpretation of hedonic regression coefficients as marginal willingness to pay for housing attributes may be overestimates, as far as the consumers are concerned and underestimates, with respect to the suppliers.

VARIABLES OF HEDONIC FUNCTION

The basic premise of the hedonic analysis is that the price of a dwelling unit is a function of various housing characteristics such as location, accessibility, size and dwelling characteristics, shelter quality, neighbourhood quality and the like.

House Prices

The dependent variable of house prices may be specified as either a flow variable (market rental values) or stock variable (prevalent market prices). In this study, stock concept, that is the market price of dwelling units, has been used. This information was obtained from the resident households and their immediate neighbours, as their own estimate of the prevalent market price of the given dwelling unit. When there was a significant deviation between these two estimates, the average of the two prices was used as the estimate of the market price of the house.

Location Variable

Variation in house prices with reference to space is observed in all cities. In the traditional analysis related to land and housing, the distance from the central business district was considered adequate to capture the variation over space. Cities, however, have a poly-nucleated structure and the employment centres are often dispersed over the entire city space. The description of Ahmedabad in the earlier chapters reveals that the city's industrial employment is concentrated in the east, the trade and commerce within the Fort walls and the service employment in west Ahmedabad. Accordingly an employment accessibility index is derived as a weighted sum of employment availability in each zone.

$$(Access)_i = \sum_{j=1}^{16} d_{ij} (E_j) \text{ for each } i = 1 \ldots\ldots 16$$

In the above formulation, E_j—is the percentage of the total city employment available in each zone and d_{ij} is the travel distance, i.e., the distance by the shortest route between a pair of zones.

The city of Ahmedabad was divided into 16 zones for this purpose, on the basis of the municipal wards. The information regarding employment available in each zone was computed from the directory of registered manufacturing units and the shops and establishments registered by the city Corporation.*

Shelter Related Variables

The size of the dwelling unit, number of rooms and age of structure are in general the variables that determine the house price. In addition, qualitative indices on a scale of 1–10 have been used for structural quality and surface quality. These are based, to a large extent, on the durability of the building materials used.

A similar index for quality of utility and services was also developed on the basis of its availability, level of services and adequacy. However, in the detailed analysis, it was seen that variables related only to the availability of services performed well and were better comprehended than an aggregate index.

Neighbourhood Characteristics Variables

In this group of variables social composition is defined as the proportion of scheduled caste/scheduled tribe population in the Census Enumeration Block as a proxy for the social mix of the neighbourhood. The physical characteristics of the neighbourhood were derived through two variables. A site quality variable which qualitatively measures the topography, density, organisation of buildings and spaces and an access quality variable related to the availability and maintenance of internal streets within the Census Block.

Tenure Security

The security of tenure essentially refers to the extent of threat of eviction or demolition of unauthorised construction. On the basis of the earlier discussion related to housing supply processes the dwelling units have been categorised as squatters, quasi-legal and formal. These have been used as dummy variables with the squatter housing as a base.

---

* In subsequent analysis, it was found that the correlation coefficient between distance from the CBD and the Employment Accessibility Index was 0.28. This highlights the fact that the traditional monocentric models of urban economy need to be modified to suit the contemporary urban structure.

RESULTS OF HEDONIC ANALYSIS

In accordance with the recognised segments of the housing market, the analysis has been undertaken separately for owners and tenants. Though in each of these, the house type variables have been included as dummy variables, separate results for slum houses and modern housing stock are also presented.

Owners

In the owner regression, the variables related to shelter size alone explain nearly 60 per cent of the variation in house prices. Within this set, the variable of rooms dominates both by its level of significance, as well as the value of coefficient. Surprisingly, the location and employment access variables do not perform well. The set of housing quality variables such as age, house type and structural or surface quality collectively increase the explanation power marginally.

Broadly, it is seen that the number of rooms within a dwelling unit significantly affects the market price and an additional room is likely to increase the price by nearly 19 per cent. There is, however, a non-linear relationship between the number of rooms and the price of the house. This, therefore, has an important implication for design of housing projects.

The tenure variables have a high coefficient value suggesting an increase of nearly 22 per cent of the price over the squatter or illegal dwelling units. In the recent slum upgradation projects, transfer of tenure rights to the present slum dwellers is generally the first step. Our finding suggests that each slum household to be benefited from the programme could be asked to pay for this expected increase in market price, charged by the transfer of ownership of plots.

It is interesting to note that there is hardly any difference between increase in prices due to quasi-legal and formal tenure. This suggests that the illegality in terms of not taking the necessary building and related permissions is of little consequence after controlling for other factors.

As regards the other housing characteristics, house size, outdoor space, structural quality, surface quality, water supply, distance from CBD and access to employment are found to be significant. However, the coefficient values indicate that their effect on house

TABLE 5.1
Regression Analysis of Hedonic Function
Dependent Variable – Log Prices

Variables	Owners	Renters
Constant	2.90651	3.34691
Shelter Related Variables		
1. Size in sq.m.	0.00267 (3.829)	0.00125 (1.43)
2. Size²	(—)	(—)
3. Additional outdoor space	0.00015 (3.926)	0.00008 (0.25)
4. Number of rooms	0.19755 (5.669)	0.19002 (1.805)
5. Room²	−0.01443 (4.196)	−0.02345 (1.01)
6. Age	0.00011 (0.124)	0.00065 (0.58)
7. Age²	(—)	(—)
Location Variables		
8. Distance	0.00033 (3.416)	−0.00027 (2.16)
9. Employment Access Index	0.00086 (2.353)	0.00152 (2.75)
House Type		
10. Chawl dummy	0.06152 (0.965)	0.04518 (0.64)
11. Pol dummy	0.03791 (0.384)	0.22347 (2.36)
12. Apt./flat dummy	0.17554 (1.850)	0.00425 (0.60)
13. Tenement/row house dummy	0.11376 (1.33)	0.31107 (3.08)
14. Bungalow dummy	0.28048 (2.7854)	0.64957 (4.94)
Services and Quality		
15. Structural quality	0.05003 (2.565)	0.04208 (2.25)
16. Surface quality	0.03432 (1.927)	−0.00975 (0.60)
17. Independent tap dummy	0.08024 (1.650)	0.04020 (0.87)
18. Independent toilet dummy	0.0895 (1.887)	0.12740 (2.76)
Neighbourhood Quality		
19. Social composition	0.02935 (0.93)	0.00489 (0.12)
20. Site quality	0.01239 (0.958)	−0.00058 (0.43)
21. Access quality	0.01370 (1.750)	0.00292 (0.39)
Tenure		
22. Quasi-legal tenure	0.21963 (2.863)	0.04667 (0.62)
23. Formal tenure	0.22792 (3.412)	−0.04792 (0.76)
Total samples	571	362
R²	0.7057	0.3890

Note: 1. (—) indicates very small coefficient values.
2. Figures in parenthesis are the t-statistics.

prices is very low, ranging from 0.3 per cent for an increase of a kilometer distance from CBD to 9 per cent for availability of private toilet. The house type dummies for apartment, bungalow on the other hand, indicate that, *ceteris paribus*, such house types command 18 to 28 per cent more price than other house types.

In consonance with an earlier hypothesis of segmentation of the housing market on the basis of house types, a separate regression analysis was undertaken for squatter and modern house types. It was found that the location variables related to distance from CBD and employment access, are significant for the squatter housing whereas the number of rooms and size variables are found to be significant for modern housing only. The services related variables are also insignificant for slum housing.

The variations between the two sets may indicate the relative housing preferences of the two distinct groups of households. For the households residing in slums, access to employment is important and they prefer to pay nearly 4 per cent more to be located closer to the place of employment. The variables related to age, structural quality and surface quality are found to be positive and significant. This suggests that the process of upgradation is taking place in informal housing and, with increase in age of the shelter, the quality of shelter is also upgraded. On the other hand, in modern housing, there is likely to be little variation on these aspects and hence they are found to be insignificant. The preferences of these households are indicated by the variables related to house size, i.e., built-up area, rooms and the availability of sanitation facilities.

Renters

On the whole, the hedonic analysis of renter housing performs poorly, with only half the explanatory power of the owner housing equation. This is largely due to the fact that the tenants were not aware of the market price of their units as well as the owners. Despite the low explanatory power, the results are remarkably similar to that of the owner housing. The shelter variable related to size and rooms initially explains 15 per cent of variations in the dependent variable. This increases dramatically to nearly 36 per cent when the house type and structural quality variable set is added. The other sets of variables related to services, neighbourhood quality and legality of tenure contribute very little to the explanatory power.

In the overall analysis, the number of rooms and house type dummies again stand out as important determinants of the value of rental houses. The major difference between the set of owners and tenants is related to the legality of tenure variable. These are found to be insignificant for rental housing. The house size variable is also not significant for rental housing. The variable reflecting availability of sanitation has a higher value for the rental housing (0.127) as compared to owner housing (0.089). Similarly employment accessibility also has a higher coefficient (0.0015) for renters as against owners (0.00086). The house type dummies for bungalows, pols and tenements have much larger coefficient values in rental equations than the owner equations.

Comparison of modern housing and slum housing indicates that the significant variables for modern housing are size and structural quality, whereas for slum housing, these are distance to CBD, age of dwelling, additional outdoor space and availability of independent water taps.

SUMMARY OF HEDONIC FUNCTION RESULTS

The underlying premise of undertaking this hedonic analysis was to highlight the fact that the market valuation of housing is based on a variety of attributes related to location, dwelling characteristics, type of dwelling, amenities and legal status.

The analysis has demonstrated the importance of certain variables like house type, number of rooms and legal status in strongly influencing the market prices. For example, in the owner equation, an additional square meter of built-up area on an average would add only Rs. 310 to the market price of the house, an increase of a room of an average size of 15 sq.mt. would add nearly Rs. 23000.*

Legal tenure also figures as an important variable in owner regression, indicating the preference of owners for dwelling units with clear titles. The coefficient of tenure variable is suggestive of the fact that when tenure rights are conferred on the slum dwellers

* In the log-linear analysis, the coefficients represent the percentage change in the dependent variable as a result of a unit change in the independent variables. These monetary estimates are derived at the mean value of the owner housing.

TABLE 5.2
Hedonic Function for Squatter and Modern Housing

	Owners		Renters	
	Modern Housing	Hutments	Modern Housing	Hutments
Constant	3.6319	2.4857	3.11328	2.9724
Distance	-0.00015 (1.12)	-0.00106 (3.96)	-0.00031 (1.59)	(—)
Emp. Access	0.00041 (0.83)	0.00411 (3.57)	0.001538 (1.42)	-0.00141 (0.99)
Age	-0.00142 (0.90)	0.01201 (2.07)	-0.00219 (0.38)	0.00510 (1.76)
Age²	(—)	-0.0007 (1.41)	(—)	(—)
Size	0.00552 (5.27)	-0.0118 (0.19)	0.009372 (3.44)	0.00496 (0.82)
Size²	(—)	(—)	(—)	(—)
Additional size	0.00046 (2.09)	0.00014 (3.99)	(—)	0.04677 (3.57)
Rooms	0.21402 (3.91)	0.38103 (1.40)	-0.2269 (1.31)	0.77804 (1.12)
Room²	-0.01624 (3.12)	-0.07083 (1.03)	0.05386 (1.58)	-0.10227 (0.53)
Structural quality	0.06721 (1.578)	0.05707 (1.92)	0.13124 (2.70)	-0.03854 (0.84)
Surface quality	0.00284 (0.001)	0.04625 (1.62)	-0.023803 (0.70)	0.06977 (1.56)
Individual water tap	0.02054 (0.22)	0.09946 (1.10)	-0.06930 (0.60)	-0.314043 (2.31)
Individual toilet	0.20065 (1.93)	-0.04870 (0.445)	0.12421 (1.22)	0.30029 (1.54)
R²	0.4536	0.6464	0.3852	0.7390
N	336	83	118	36

Note: (—) Indicates very small coefficient values.
Figures in parenthesis are the t-statistics.

through the Slum Improvement Programme, the market value is likely to go up by nearly 22 per cent.

The hedonic analysis also highlights the preferences of actors in various sub-markets. The tenant group in general and the slum dwellers in particular, exhibit a higher preference for location near employment centres, whereas owners residing in modern housing do not consider this to be important. For them, the size of the house and the number of rooms in the house are more important aspects of housing. The type of shelter is an important determinant of house prices and modern housing with all amenities is preferred both by owner and renter groups.

Though, as indicated earlier, these implicit prices reflect the consumers' as well as suppliers' bid-rent functions for specific attributes, they provide sufficient guidelines for understanding th underlying preference structure of different actors in the various sub-markets. Such an understanding can help in design of new housing programmes and projects as well as help in evaluating the existing programmes.

Expenditure on Housing in Ahmedabad

The residents of Ahmedabad appear to spend relatively small amounts on housing. The mean housing expenditure is Rs. 114, with a median expenditure at Rs. 53. The monthly housing expenditure is defined as the actual out-of-pocket expenditure on housing. In case of renters, this includes rents, taxes and maintenance expenditure, if any. For owners, the housing expenditure relates to taxes, maintenance expenditure and the payments towards borrowed capital and interest thereof. The poorer households in Ahmedabad spend a much larger proportion of their income on housing. The poorest households spend on an average 18 per cent of their income on housing as against the richer households who spend a mere 7 per cent.

The low levels of housing expenditure can be partly explained through the low rents for tenants due to the Rent Control Legislation. As elaborated earlier, nearly 50 per cent of the households in Ahmedabad Municipal Corporation area have been staying in their present house for at least fifteen years. The average age of the housing stock is also about twenty years. The owners of this housing stock also spend only a small amount each month towards taxes, as the city's property tax structure overwhelmingly favours the owners, since assessment of the annual rentable value of owner occupied property is done on the basis of extremely low rates on the capital value of the property existing at the time of construction.

Out-of-pocket expenditure on housing does not capture the 'true' nature of housing expenditure since it does not take into account the initial downpayments made by the households. To take cognisance of such large payments the housing expenditure has been estimated as inclusive of out-of-pocket expenses, as well as the implicit interest of 12 per cent per annum on the amount paid at the initial stage.

With this implicit housing expenditure, it is seen that the owner households spend nearly two and a half times more than the renter households. The premium attached to ownership of a house is a reflection of the fact that housing is also considered an investment good and, given the likely capital gains, owners are willing to spend a little more for similar houses as compared to the renters.

Housing Expenditure-Income Ratio

The above discussion can best be understood by examining the rent-income ratios for the renters and the housing expenditure-income ratios for the owners. With a heterogeneous housing market beset with rent control legislations, it is apparent that within each income class, we would find a substantial variation in the rent to income ratios. In order to present a more meaningful and discernible picture of housing expenditure, the median rent-income ratios for each income class is shown in Table 5.3.

One of the important results that emerges from Table 5.3 is that housing expenditure to monthly income ratios for both owners and renters are quite small. While renters, on an average, spend 15 per cent of their monthly income on housing, the owners spend as little as 8 per cent of their monthly income on current housing expenditure. If the interest loss due to downpayment is included, then the owners on an average, are found to spend 22 per cent of their income on housing.

If the median rent-income ratio of each class is examined separately, it is seen that the rent-income ratio has a skewed distribution. Looking at the median value of rent-income ratio, half of the

TABLE 5.3

Median Housing Expenditure—Household Income Ratio by Income Groups

Income Groups	Total Sample		Owners		Renters	
(Rupees per month)	*Owner*	*Renter*	*Median for*			
			Exp-1 ÷ Income	*Exp-2 ÷ Income*	*Exp-1 ÷ Income*	*Exp-2 ÷ Income*
Less than 750	138	131	0.050	0.157	0.131	0.131
750 to 1000	71	85	0.026	0.070	0.089	0.090
1000 to 1500	92	70	0.065	0.218	0.047	0.050
1500 to 2000	71	35	0.036	0.086	0.047	0.047
2000 to 2500	40	22	0.043	0.167	0.020	0.020
2500 to 3000	30	6	0.053	0.171 ⎫	0.032	0.032
3000 to 3500	23	3	0.027	0.070 ⎭		
3500 to 4000	14	8	0.027	0.087 ⎫	0.050	0.050
4000 or more	52	2	0.023	0.049 ⎭		
Total	531	362				
Median			0.040	0.120	0.075	0.076
Mean			0.083	0.220	0.150	0.150

Note: Housing Expenditure 1 (Renters) = Rent + taxes + maintenance.
Housing Expenditure 1 (Owners) = Monthly instalments + taxes + maintenance.
Housing Expenditure 2 (Renters) = (HE 1) + (0.01 × (Key money).
Housing Expenditure 2 (Owners) = (HE 1) + (0.01 × (Down payment).

renter households in Ahmedabad spend less than 8 per cent of income on rents. Correspondingly, half the owners in Ahmedabad spend only 4 per cent of their income on current housing expenditure, inclusive of imputed value. The results are consistent with those obtained for other developing countries as shown in Table 5.4

The second important aspect to be noted from Table 5.3 is with regard to the general decline in the rent-income ratio with increase in income. This suggests that the income elasticity of housing demand is positive and less than one and the lower income household spend a larger proportion of their income on housing as compared to higher income households. While a consistent decline in rent-income ratio for renters is noticed the owners' information is highly erratic as far as current expenditure is concerned—indicating a weaker relationship between current housing expenditure-

TABLE 5.4
Rent-Income Ratios for Developing Countries

City	Owner	Renter
Colombia		
Bogota	0.20	0.18
Cali	0.17	0.19
Egypt		
Benisuef	0.18	0.09
Cairo	0.10	0.07
El Salvador		
Santa Ana	0.10	0.08
Somsonate	0.24	0.08
Korea		
Seoul	0.40	0.22
Busan	0.41	0.16
Phillipines		
Davao	0.04	0.08
Manila	0.27	0.09
Jamaica		
Kingston	—	0.27
India		
Bangalore	0.25	0.10
Ahmedabad	0.12	0.08

Source: Malpezzi et al. (1985).
Note: Information related to Ahmedabad is from our sample study.

income ratio and income of the household. For the imputed expenditure, the median rent-income ratio seems to increase initially and decline beyond the income of Rs. 1500. It is also observed that the two columns of renters are almost identical. This suggests that only some of the renters in the city have paid key money. (Fig. 5.1 gives a schematic presentation of the variation in income and expenditure-income ratio.)

It has been earlier argued that there are distinct segments of the metropolitan housing market. Such market segmentation could best be understood through the type of shelter as each type appears to cater to a particular client group. It thus, becomes necessary to examine the housing expenditure pattern across the house types to discern certain useful insights into the sub-market characteristics. Tables 5.5 and 5.6, give the median rent-income ratios by house types for various income categories.

For both owners and renters, the median rent-income ratios decline with an increase in income, irrespective of the house type.

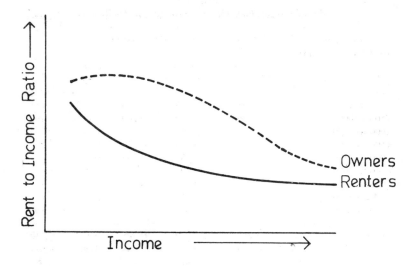

FIGURE 5.1 : Median Rent to Income Ratio for Renters and Owners

TABLE 5.5
Housing Expenditure-Income by House Type for Owners

Monthly Income (Rupees per month)	Median Expenditure-2/Income for				
	Bungalow/ Row House	Apartment/ Tenement	Pol	Chawl	Hut
Less than 750	0.388	0.574	0.02	0.175	0.050
750 to 1000	0.150	0.525	0.015	0.083	0.012
1000 to 1500	0.046	0.395	0.035	0.068	0.015
1500 to 2000	0.046	0.282	0.020	0.024	—
2000 to 2500	0.094	0.225	0.015	0.150	—
2500 to 3000	0.175	0.185	0.020	—	—
3000 to 3500	0.050	0.150	—	—	—
3500 to 4000	0.075	0.200	0.060	—	—
4000 or more	0.092	0.075	0.016	—	—
Mean	0.209	0.288	0.064	0.125	0.125
Median	0.111	0.270	0.018	0.068	0.0425
N	131	202	59	56	83

Note: For the Exp-2 specification see Table 5.4

TABLE 5.6
Housing Expenditure-Income by House Type for Renters

Monthly Income (Rupees per month)	Median Rent/Income for				
	Bungalow/ Row House	Apartment/ Tenement	Pol	Chawl	Hut
Less than 750	0.666	0.125	0.119	0.113	0.153
750 to 1000	0.666	0.150	0.040	0.086	0.100
1000 to 1500	0.018	0.090	0.075	0.040	0.023
1500 to 2000	—	0.138	0.020	0.015	—
2000 to 2500	—	0.035	0.035	0.015	—
2500 to 3000	—	0.010	—	0.035	—
3000 to 3500	—	0.035	0.035	—	—
3500 to 4000	—	0.015	—	—	—
4000 or more	—	—	—	—	—
Mean	0.244	0.118	0.075	0.137	0.130
Median	0.100	0.097	0.044	0.067	0.087
N	22	96	49	159	36

It must, however, be noted that those ratios are higher for bungalows, flats and tenements. For example, an owner of an apartment
spends nearly 29 per cent of his monthly income on housing as
compared to 13 per cent for the slum owner. A tenant household
in an apartment, however, pays only 12 per cent of his monthly
income as rent, whereas tenants in chawls and slums spend 13 per
cent of their income on housing (Table 5.6). It can be deduced
from this that the rent control legislations largely appear to favour
tenants of apartments/tenements; the mean and median ratios for
the other house types for tenants are generally similar or greater
for the tenants as compared to the owners.

One of the important findings of this analysis is that with 'better'
shelter quality, the housing expenditure to income ratio also
increases. This implies that even at the same income level, households are potentially willing to pay a much larger proportion of the
income for a better shelter quality. The conventional approach in
designing public housing programmes for lower income groups
instead assumes certain fixed affordability levels. In the design of
the new housing schemes for the lower income groups, it is thus
likely that the poorer households would be willing to pay substantially more than their present housing expenditure for a better
shelter quality, provided that its location is appropriate.

Housing Demand Analysis

Conventional demand analysis postulates a relationship between the quantity of a good demanded, its relative price, the income of the household and other demographic characteristics affecting demand. In this perspective, one can identify,

$$Q_h = f (P_h, Y, Z_1, Z_2, Z_3.....) \quad (1)$$

Where Q_h is the quantity of housing services demanded, P_h is the relative price of housing and Z_1 (i = 1....n) are the household characteristics. With regard to housing demand analysis, there are crucial issues of measurement of the variables, particularly Q_h, P_h and Y as well as functional form of the equation. These problems are briefly discussed below.

Measurement of Dependent Variable

In the available literature on the measurement of the dependent variable related to quantity of housing consumed, it is common to use expenditure on housing, in the form of rents paid as a surrogate for consumption (Malpezzi and Mayo, 1985). The rent R is, however, a product of unit price and quantity consumed; and the relation postulated above now becomes,

$$R = P_h Q_h = f (P_h, Y, Z_i) \ldots \quad (2)$$

Depending upon one's notion of the housing services bundle, the price variable will vary for each household if it is related only to shelter size or be constant for a sub-market, when housing is defined broadly to include shelter, neighbourhood characteristics and access. In consonance with our approach related to hedonic equations, the price variable has been included as constant for a sub-market. The relationship thus becomes,

$$R = \bar{P}_h Q_h = f (\bar{P}_h, Y, Z_i) \ldots . \quad (3)$$

In empirical analysis, there are difficulties associated with measurement of rents for owners and those tenants who paid a lump-sum payment initially. An added difficulty pertains to consideration of gross rent (inclusive of payments of taxes, utilities) or net rent (exclusive payment for shelter). The concept of gross rental payments has been used for renter households. These rental values are imputed for any large key money payment at 1 per cent of value per month. A similar procedure is adopted for owner households. In addition to their monthly housing expenditure, which includes repayment of borrowed capital, the imputed value of the downpayment has been included at 1 per cent of its value. This procedure of computing housing consumption for owners is different from the mainstream literature, where imputed rents from the market value of owner housing is used. For example, Malpezzi et al. (1985) have used 'either (i) net imputed rents based on owners' imputations, (ii) predicted rent from a hedonic price regression, or (iii) imputed value from a fixed amortisation rate to owners' estimate of housing value'.

We feel that the use of imputed rental values in the demand analysis for owners is likely to give an upward bias in the estimates of income elasticity. This is largely because housing is typically viewed by owners not only as a consumption good but also as an asset of a potential future income in the form of capital gains. In a housing market like Ahmedabad, where house prices probably increased rapidly during the seventies, the asset demand component of housing for the owners is likely to be considerable. Further, in a market, where rents are controlled due to legislation, imputing the rental value of owner housing and using it in the expenditure analysis, is likely to generate misleading results. Thus, in order to maintain compatibility with the renter households' estimation, the notion of imputed gross housing expenditure for owner households has been adopted.

Housing Price Measurement

The problems associated with measurement of housing consumption and housing price are closely related. In equation (3), it was suggested that housing price variable, P_h can be constant for a sub-market. Most studies of housing demand have assumed a constant price throughout the sample and hence omitted the price term. This omission, often on account of non-availability of information, can be serious as it may bias other demand equation parameters if the omitted price term is correlated with other variables. This is particularly true if a single linear expenditure equation is used for estimation.

A few research studies that include the price variable (e.g., King and Mieszkowski (1973) and Polinsky and Elwood, 1979) have allowed the intra-metropolitan prices to vary across neighbourhoods or by dwelling units. Such a specification may again wrongly state the price variation in the sample, if households are not limited in their choice to specific neighbourhoods or dwelling units. Mayo (1983), in a study of housing demand in Egypt, uses land price variations as a surrogate for housing price.

In this study, we have followed Ingram's logic of identifying a housing price variable on the basis of the available information regarding the various market segmentations in the city. Accordingly, we have treated the five zones of the city and the tenure status (i.e., owners and renters) in each of these five zones as distinct sub-markets. The hedonic analysis, presented in the earlier section was undertaken for these sub-markets.

$$Pij = b_o + \sum_k b_k x_k$$

where, Pij is the market price of 'ith' tenure class in 'jth' zone and x_k are the dwelling characteristics.

We then use the sample wide average of the housing attributes as representing a standardised bundle of housing services and estimate the price of this standardised bundle for each zone. Each of this zone in Ahmedabad represents a distinct characteristic of the housing market, either through preponderance of a dominant house type or through concentration of a particular income class. In the context of Ahmedabad at least, it thus appears to be correct to assume that households residing in a particular zone operate within a specific zonal market.

Functional Form of Demand Equation

Linear expenditure functions are most often used in modelling based on system of demand equations, where the functional form satisfies certain criteria required for system-wide consistency of price and income elasticity estimates. The linear function is moreover, consistent with Stone-Geary utility function— implying that it has theoretically appealing properties and permits explicit derivation of the parameters of the underlying utility function (Mayo, 1978).

The linear form is, however, restrictive in the sense that the income and price elasticities measured through it are constrained to increase or decrease monotonically as prices and incomes change. The log-linear form, on the other hand, provides estimates of constant elasticities that are independent of levels of income, prices or demographic variables. Hence, while the log-linear form provides useful summary information about general behaviour, it does not allow us to measure the variations.

Empirical Results

In the empirical analysis, in addition to income and price variables, many other variables which may have an influence on housing demand have been included. The analysis is presented separately for linear (Table 5.7) and log-linear equations (Table 5.8). From the R-Square statistics, it is apparent that the log-linear model is better suited for both renters and owners. It is possible to compare the two R-squared statistics as the dependent variable in each case is estimated in a similar manner. However, though the log-linear model provides a better fit, it also gives lower estimates of income elasticities for renter households, and a slightly higher income elasticity for owner households. The price elasticity estimate is thus the coefficient of the price term minus one.

TABLE 5.7
Linear Demand Analysis
Dependent Variable: Imputed Housing Expenditure per Month

Variables	Renters	Owners	Pooled
Intercept	225.3109	71.4952	118.4616
Income	0.0482 (3.274)	0.0323 (2.646)	0.0324 (3.431)
Age of Head	−0.8753 (0.978)	−0.6668 (0.398)	−0.4030 (0.369)
Household Size	−13.5712 (3.558)	−4.3883 (0.953)	−5.8640 (1.781)
State in Life Cycle	−15.8155 (2.148)	−16.0487 (1.093)	0.3583 (0.382)
Commitment to City	−34.6226 (1.791)	−67.8852 (1.654)	−60.607 (2.362)
Duration of Residence	−0.5675 (0.815)	−8.1659 (5.889)	−5.4034 (6.098)
Dependents/Earner	0.5913 (0.111)	3.0353 (0.295)	2.8503 (0.441)
Formal Sector Job Dummy	10.5234 (0.578)	55.5876 (1.957)	35.5126 (1.489)
Tenure Security	0.3333 (1.127)	1.6463 (1.651)	1.1293 (2.406)
Price	0.0009 (2.172)	0.0017 (4.823)	0.0018 (8.722)
N	362	531	893
R-square	0.147	0.245	0.25
Elasticities at mean			
Income	0.428	0.189	0.21
Price	−0.787	−0.382	−0.392

TABLE 5.8
Log-Linear Demand Analysis
Dependent Variable: Log of Imputed Housing Expenditure per Month

Variables	Renters	Owners	Pooled
Intercept	1.1937	−1.547	−0.528
Log Income	0.1677 (1.955)	0.2041 (2.671)	0.1942 (3.375)
Age of Head	−0.0010 (0.385)	−0.0001 (0.053)	0.0005 (0.282)
Household size	−0.0334 (3.031)	−0.0028 (0.463)	−0.0102 (1.905)
Stage in			
Life cycle	−0.0305 (1.368)	0.0509 (2.528)	0.0079 (0.518)
Commitment to City	−0.1960 (3.338)	−0.1106 (1.951)	−0.1638 (3.923)
Duration of			
Residence	−0.0089 (4.264)	−0.0182 (9.638)	−0.0153 (10.645)
Dependents/Earner	−0.1763 (1.155)	0.0285 (2.024)	0.0093 (0.884)
Formal Sector Job	0.0419 (0.749)	0.1235 (2.341)	0.0933 (2.361)
Tenure Security	0.0007 (0.787)	0.0031 (2.014)	0.0019 (2.543)
Log Price	0.1633 (2.109)	0.5683 (5.997)	0.4383 (8.761)
N	362	531	893
R-Square	0.219	0.403	0.336
Elasticities:			
Income	0.167	0.204	0.194
Price	−0.834	−0.432	−0.562

Note: For estimation of price elasticity,
$$\text{Log } Q_h = a + E_y \log Y + E_p \log P$$
$$\text{Log } R = \log Q_h P_h = a + E_y \log Y + (1+E_p) \log P.$$

Income Elasticity

Mayo (1983), Malpezzi et al. (1985), and others have identified through a survey of literature on housing demand in developing countries, that the income elasticities of demand among renters are generally small (to the order of 0.3 to 0.6); income elasticities of demand among owners are somewhat larger (to the order of 0.4 to 0.8), and that these results are generally consistent with findings for developed countries. Our results, however, indicate the income elasticity of demand among renters to be in the range of 0.17 to 0.43 (depending upon the functional form used) and for the owners it is around 0.20.

While the literature presents higher income elasticity of demand for owners, it essentially looks at asset demand because the housing consumption expenditure in most studies represent the implicit rental values of owner housing based on the market price.* However, with such formulations, it becomes difficult to compare the owner and renter demand behaviour, because the dependent variables are not comparable. As mentioned earlier, our study does not suffer from this lacunae because the housing consumption estimates for both owner and renter households are compatible.

The income elasticity estimates in the region of 0.2 to 0.4 for both owner and renter households indicate a largely inelastic demand for housing. To explore household behaviour further, a separate analysis for different income groups was carried out, the results of which are presented in Table 5.9. This shows that for low-income households, the income elasticity of demand is negative,

TABLE 5.9
Income Elasticities for Various Income Groups

	Linear	*Log-linear*	*Samples*
Renters			
Low income			
(less than Rs. 700)	−0.938	−0.69	(105)
Middle income			
(Rs. 700 to 1500)	0.207	0.057	(165)
High income			
(Rs. 1500 and above)	0.571	0.362	(92)
All Renters	0.428	0.167	(362)
Owners			
Low income	-0.515	−0.048	(126)
Middle Income	0.763	0.546	(175)
High Income	0.313	0.208	(230)
All Owners	0.189	0.204	(531)

Note: All elasticities are computed at the Mean for Linear equation.

implying proportionate decrease in housing expenditure for both owners and renters, with increase in income. This result, surprising in the light of the international evidence, is logical, as housing is probably a lower priority for the households in low income group. Here again, it is interesting to note the significant difference in the estimates of income elasticities between the linear and log-linear

---

* Our own analysis, using the amortised value, at 1 per cent of the estimated market value, as the housing consumption expenditure for owner households, yielded an estimate of income elasticity of demand at the mean at 0.48.

models. The log-linear models, which are a better fit to the data, suggest a value close to zero for poor owner and renter households, implying a perfect income inelasticity of housing demand.

The linear demand function which implies a monotonic increase in income elasticities appears to hold true only for renters, whereas for owner households, a much higher income elasticity of demand is noticed for the middle income households than for the high income households. Though the elasticity estimates in log-linear model are smaller, similar trend of higher income elasticity of demand for middle income owner households is apparent.

Fig. 5.2 gives a schematic presentation of the variations in income elasticity of demand for different income groups. The renter households' demand behaviour indicates an increasing income elasticity with income. It must, however, be noted that (at least in the log-linear equation) the increase in income elasticity of renters for middle income households is very marginal.

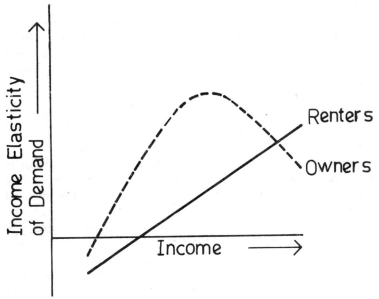

FIGURE 5.2   :   Income Elasticity of Demand by Income

This rather inelastic nature of rental housing demand for lower and middle income households is probably on account of the prevailing rent control legislation, which does not allow for an increase in rents. Among the higher income tenants, the presence of a few households paying monthly rents of more than Rs, 500, have probably affected the income elasticity estimates. On the other hand, the middle income owners, from the above estimates, appear to attach a high priority to house ownership and are likely to spend more than 50 per cent of the increases in income towards housing (income elasticity 0.54 in log-linear equation).

Price Elasticity of Demand

The estimates of price elasticity of demand for renters are around -0.8 and for owner households around -0.4. The renter households essentially pay for the housing services that they consume today and it is thus quite likely that their housing consumption would decline in nearly the same proportion as the increase in price. The owner households, on the other hand, not only consume the housing services but also view housing as a durable asset with positive capital gains and thus have a higher (algebraic) price elasticity than renters.

These price elasticity estimates are consistent with the other estimates for Egypt and Philippines presented in Malpezzi (1985) which indicate that a rental housing programme with public sector subsidy is likely to induce a higher level of housing consumption than the owner housing programme with public subsidies.

Effect of Other Variables on the Housing Market

The log-linear models (which have a better fit to the data) indicate that the household size, urban commitment and duration of residence are the other significant variables for tenant households in addition to the income and price variables discussed above. The negative sign for household sizes is contrary to the hypothesised positive effect on housing consumption of those variables. The impact of urban commitment variable indicates that a household head with an intention to return 'home' spends nearly 20 per cent less on housing.

The variable duration of residence has the expected negative sign, indicating effect of rent control. However, the magnitude of the coefficient suggests a decrease of only one per cent per year of residence. Thus, on an average, the impact of rent control legislation on the household's consumption of housing is only marginal.

The negative sign of the household size variable is reflective of the constraints faced by the households in the housing market that, despite larger household size, they may be constrained to decrease their housing consumption, often by changing the family consumption basket rather than moving in to a bigger house. These issues are discussed further in the next chapter.

Owner households' housing consumption appears to be independent of the size of the family. It is, instead, related to the households' stage in the life cycle. With each stage of the life cycle, the owner households, on an average, increase housing consumption by nearly 5 per cent. The negative sign of duration of residence variable suggests, as in the case of renters, that the benefits of the large scale supply through housing cooperative societies in the sixties and seventies have probably accrued to these households.

Owner households with assured incomes as, for example, from a formal sector job, spend nearly 12 per cent more than households whose income sources are uncertain. The dummy variable on formal sector jobs is construed as a proxy for 'permanent income' and, as indicated in the housing demand literature, the permanent income elasticity of demand is generally higher than the current income elasticity of demand. The high coefficient of this formal sector dummy variable corroborates the importance of permanent income in housing demand analysis. The high coefficient of the formal sector dummy also suggests an easier access to institutional housing finance, which is generally linked to the regularity in repayment capabilities. In this perspective, the formal sector employees, who have easier access to institutional housing finance, are likely to consume more housing than the informal sector workers.

Premium on Ownership

The premium paid for ownership can be examined through the ratio of the opportunity cost of owning present housing and the gross imputed housing expenditure. The opportunity cost of housing is derived as 1 per cent of the estimated capital gains on the potential sale of house.* Table 5.10 presents the ratio of the

* To get a correct assessment of the opportunity cost, we have substracted the initial down payments, if any, from the owners' estimate of the sale price of the house. This capital gain accruing notionally to the owner is valued at a conservative rate of 12 per cent per year (1 per cent per month). This is a rate of return available in India on Government sponsored savings schemes like National Savings Certificate and the Public Provident Fund Schemes.

TABLE 5.10

Ownership Premia Paid by Owners of Different Sub-markets
(Mean ratio of opportunity cost on capital gains and imputed housing expenditure)

Housing Type	Income Class			All Owners
	Low	Medium	High	
	(Less than 700)	(Rs. 700 to 1500)	(More than Rs. 1500)	
Formal	11.94	19.56	27.95	23.10
	(2.82)	(6.35)	(5.12)	(3.46)
Informal	9.24	8.58	14.52	9.71
	(2.18)	(1.50)	(4.84)	(1.32)

Note: Figures in parenthesis are standard errors.

imputed value of capital gains to the current imputed housing expenditure by owners. It is apparent from this analysis that owners in Ahmedabad pay a large premium for ownership, both in informal and formal housing markets.

This large implicit premia indicates that, if the formal sector owners were to sell their house today and invest the sale amount in Government security, they would on an average, almost double their monthly earnings. The standard errors of the ratios presented in Table 5.10, indicate that for many households, the implicit increase in monthly incomes will be even more than double.

A relevant question to raise here is that given this fact why do owner households (particularly those in the lower and middle income groups) not encash this opportunity of raising their income substantially? Two important explanations of such behaviour relate to the nature of housing supply processes and the nature of asset demand of housing. It is likely that many households find it difficult and expensive to buy new housing. The information levels in any case are also extremely poor. The housing situation, especially for owner households is more likely to be very close to the 'desired' housing situation, and that there may be a great resistance on the part of the household members to alter it. These aspects related to households' preferences and constraints are discussed in the next chapter.

More importantly, owner households today view housing as an asset and are willing to pay the large implicit premium to capitalise it in the event of a need arising at a future date. In this context, the premia indicates the potential willingness to pay for home ownership, and if adequate housing finances were made available, the average propensity to spend on housing would see a voluntary increase. For the informal sector, particularly, these premia indicate that owners are likely to spend more on programmes of tenure reform and upgradation.

Summary

In our descriptive analysis of housing expenditure, it was found that the mean monthly expenditure on housing in Ahmedabad was Rs. 114 with 50 per cent households spending less than Rs. 53 per month. The proportion of total income spent on housing declined with increasing income, with the poorest group (income less than Rs. 750) spending nearly 18 per cent of their monthly income on housing and the richer group (income more than Rs. 2000) spending only 7 per cent on housing.

The median rent-income ratio decreases monotonically with income for renters. It, however, increases initially for owners with increases in income and then declines subsequently with increasing income. Thus the marginal propensity to spend on ownership for the middle-income household appears to be quite high. The same results are better understood with an analysis of housing demand. The income elasticity of demand for owners is 0.2 and in the region of 0.17 to 0.40 for tenants, depending upon the functional form of the demand equation. This suggests a generally inelastic housing demand. However, when the income elasticity of demand for various income groups is examined, it is observed that for lower- and middle-income tenants, the income elasticity of demand is close to zero, and rises to 0.36 for higher income renters. On the other hand, for the owner household, the income elasticity is as high as 0.70 for the middle-income households.

These elasticity estimates suggest that with adequate supply of housing finance, one would expect a much larger spending on the part of middle income households. The 'success' of financial institutions like the Housing Finance Development Corporation which provide financial assistance to middle-income households highlights this fact. The near inelastic demand for both renters and owners in the lower income groups suggest that in the absence of subsidies from public agencies, they are unlikely to increase their housing consumption. However, the rent-income ratio across house types for the lower-income groups, was found to increase with better house types. This suggests a potential willingness to pay more for better housing, even amongst the poorer households.

TABLE A5.1
Means for Variables for Hedonic Analysis

Variables		Mean and Standard Deviation	
		Owners	*Renters*
Size			
1. Total built-up area of dwelling unit in sq.mts.	HOUSESZ	65.66 (67.75)	31.19 (66.77)
2. Square of house size	HSZSQ	8894.58 (25016.1)	5418.9 (48361.4)
3. Additional outdoor space, if any, in sq.mts.	ADDSP	55.15 (380.90)	7.62 (62.83)
4. Number of rooms including kitchen	ROOMS	3.08 (1.95)	1.64 (0.80)
5. Square of rooms	RMSQ	13.35 (17.70)	3.34 (3.55)
Location			
6. Distance to city centre in meters	DIST	400.63 (193.40)	388.23 (230.37)
7. Scores for employment accessibility (see text)	EMPSC	148.36 (49.28)	144.38 (46.82)
Shelter Quality			
8. Age of dwelling in years	AGE	49.99 (135.38)	50.40 (115.65)
9. Square of age	AGESQ	20795.9 (137096.6)	15878.4 (116426.8)
Dummy variables for house type with hutments as base			
10. Dummy for chawls	CHAWLD	0.156	0.439
11. Dummy for pols	POLD	0.110	0.135
12. Dummy for apartments and flats	APTD	0.126	0.127
13. Dummy for row house and tenements	TEND	0.338	0.163
14. Dummy for bungalows	BUNGD	0.121	0.036
15. Structural quality of dwelling (scores developed from wall and roof quality and structural condition—see text)	STRUQ	9.70 (1.72)	9.01 (1.69)
16. Surface quality of dwelling (scores developed from exterior conditions of wall finishing, flooring and opening—see text)	SURFQ	7.66 (1.73)	6.67 (1.81)
17. Dummy variable for an independent tap	TAPD	0.819	0.644
18. Dummy variable for an independent toilet	TOILD	0.720	0.464

Table A5.1 *contd.*

Variables		Mean and Standard Deviation	
		Owners	Renters
Neighbourhood			
19. *Social composition* Proportion of scheduied caste/ tribe population in the Census enumeration block	SOC	0.646 (0.478)	0.588 (0.493)
20. *Site quality* (Scores developed from the site conditions like topography. density, organisation of spaces, and buildings)	SITQ	7.046 (1.709)	6.74 (3.58)
21. *Access quality* (Scores based on the quality of internal streets and their maintenance within the Census enumeration block)	ACCQ	12.21 (2.467)	12.26 (6.43)
Tenure Dummy variables with squatters- illegal occupation of land as base			
22. Dummy variable for quasi- legal tenure (Legal occupation of land but permissions for buildings not taken)	QLEGD	0.051	0.179
23. Dummy variable for formal tenure (Both legal occupation of land and buildings with the necessary permission)	FORTEND	0.779	0.613
24. Dependent variable log of occupant's estimate of price of dwelling (see text)	LOGPR	4.757 (0.600)	4.257 (0.419)
Sample Size (N)		571	362

Note: Figures in parenthesis are standard deviations.

TABLE A5.2
Means for Variables in Demand Analysis
(Pooled Sample—N = 933)

Variables		Mean and Standard Deviation
1. Household income—Gross for all sources	HHINC	1589.29 (1489.25)
2. Age of head of household in completed years	AGE	40.42 (13.03)
3. Household size	HHSIZE	6.20 (3.77)
4. Stage in life cycle (for detailed discription - see Table A6.1)	STLIFE	4.08 (1.47)
5. Dummy variable for urban commitment (= 1 if head of household indicated an intention to return 'home')	RETURN	0.53
6. Duration of residence in current dwelling—in years	DURRES	20.32 (15.41)
7. Number of dependents per earner in the household	DEP	2.92 (1.92)
8. Dummy variable for employment of head of household in the formal sector (Employer or employee in an establishment with more than 10 workers)	FORSEC	0.50
9. Security of tenure	TENSEC	82.53 (30.05)
10. Estimated housing price faced in the market (see text)	HSEPR	83273.88 (71420.71)
11. Housing expenditure (Rupees per month)	HEXP	245.03 (401.97)

Note: Figures in parenthesis are standard deviations.

6. Housing Preferences and Constraints

The analysis of housing demand in the previous chapter was essentially based on an assumption of a 'perfect' housing market. In this type of micro economic analysis 'the consumer is assumed to choose among the alternatives available to him or her in such a manner that the satisfaction derived from consuming commodities (in the broadest sense) is as large as possible' (Jones, 1979). The only constraint that is explicitly recognised in such choice based models is that of the household budget. We now attempt to view housing preferences in a different perspective. It is recognised that only some households, who are satisfied with their housing, may be considered to be in a state of equilibrium. The differences between these households and others are analysed to understand housing preferences. The importance is not placed only on choice and household budget. Housing preferences are treated in qualitative rather than only monetary terms; specific attention is also paid to 'the role which low incomes and the structure of the housing market play in constraining decisions' (Edwards, 1983). Other constraints like access to finance and institutional measures are also examined. It becomes necessary to pay attention to these in situations where these factors are more important than voluntary choices on the basis of individual tastes and preferences. In India where conditions like acute housing and land shortage exist along with inaccessibility to financial assistance, worsening income distribution pattern, dwindling public sector resources and unpredictable political attitudes, it is likely that the housing markets are riddled with constraints and are highly segmented. Any inquiry into household residential behaviour in such situations must recognise the predominance of these constraints.

Conceptual Basis

The tenure preferences among different households are more likely to depend upon the stage in the life cycle and social background whereas preferred house size may depend upon the household size and previous housing situations. One of the major determinants of housing preferences is the socio-demographic and economic background of households.

In keeping with the recognition of housing as a bundle of different services, housing preferences are also viewed as multi-dimensional. Further, unlike the assumptions in most micro-economic models which envisage 'instantaneous response to infinitely small price variations', the real world household behaviour is probably subject to thresholds. The existence of such thresholds implies that each household has a zone of indifference within which housing prices and/or satisfaction levels with different attributes are not likely to induce significant change in the utility derived. In operational terms, this implies that on each dimension of housing attribute, upper and lower limits may be defined. These boundaries define the aspiration region of a given household (Brown and Moore, 1970). Further, a given household also has differing priorities for different elements. Thus, for example, at an advanced stage in the life cycle the highest priority may be for owning a house. The priorities may be reflected in the limited range of the aspiration region.

Besides the socio-demographic determinants, the households continually adjust their preferences and aspiration regions in response to their perception of affordability for housing and the perceived housing opportunities and prices. Although conceptually it is possible to distinguish between the initial and adjusted aspiration regions, it is difficult to identify these for any given household as the adjustments occur as a dynamic and on-going process. The perception of affordability depends on three important factors, the possibility, extent and terms of financial assistance for housing and the household's awareness regarding these; the household's own income and savings; and its perception regarding the stream of earnings in the near future. Similarly, the perception of housing opportunities and prices depends simultaneously on the available opportunities and prevailing prices in relation to the aspiration region and, more importantly, the household's awareness regarding these depending on their action, space and information channels. These aspects are schematically presented in Fig. 6.1.

Thus, the aspiration region of housing attributes is jointly determined by the three sets of determinants, the socio-demographic

FIGURE 6.1 : Housing Preferences and Aspiration Regions

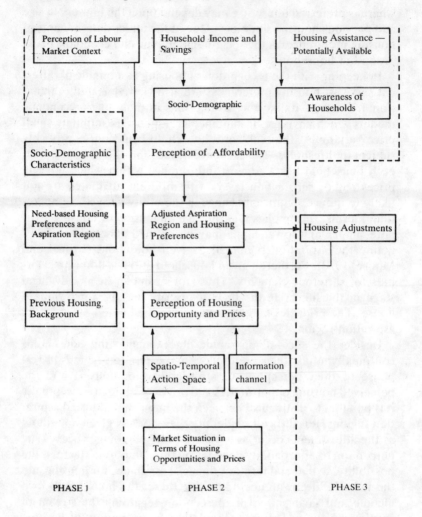

and economic characteristics, perception of affordability and perception of housing opportunities and prices. The utility derived from a given housing situation depends on the extent to which it lies within the aspiration region of the household and its preference ranking of different housing attributes.

The second important aspect of residential behaviour relates to the need for and the process of housing adjustments. The need for an adjustment may arise from changes in any of the three sets of determinants, which may result in a mismatch between the present housing attributes and the aspiration region. One such example may be a change in household size. The resultant requirement for additional space will generate a stress and the new aspiration region may put the present house outside these limits. However, this revision in the aspiration region will also be partially determined by the household's perception of affordability and available housing opportunities. Alternatively, an increased supply of a particular type of housing may lead to a complete change in the perception of opportunity and a revision in the aspiration region without any change in needs. Similarly, an increased potential of financial assistance for housing may also create such dynamic reconsiderations.

The major implication here is that those households with limited perceptions of affordability and opportunity are not likely to even try for any change in their housing situations. This will, of course, also be true in situations of highly constrained local housing markets with housing shortages, high and rising prices and weak information flow. In such situations the households will more likely adjust their needs rather than attempt any housing adjustment.

On the whole then, we may conclude that a household will contemplate change if the difference in utility from a perceived affordable opportunity and the utility from the current housing situation is higher than the costs associated with making this change. These include both the transaction costs (actual and psychological) and the differentials in housing expenditure between the two situations.

Analytical Approach

It is extremely difficult to derive housing preferences directly. One of the ways generally adopted is to study the recent movers to understand the determinants of mobility and in turn revealing the underlying housing preferences. However, the rates of recent mobility in Ahmedabad are very low. Only 2.3 per cent of the households had moved within the last two years and 8.4 per cent in the last five years. It is difficult to derive any meaningful analysis from such a small sample. Further, beyond this time span, recall problems would severely limit the quality of data for a detailed understanding of housing preferences and constraints. We have, therefore, adopted two different approaches. The first one, which is basically cross-sectional, examines the preferences and constraints in detail by distinguishing households in terms of their satisfaction with their housing. The second approach relies on the more traditional housing career perspective by looking at the past residential mobility and housing upgradation processes. These housing adjustments are examined in the next chapter.

In the cross-sectional approach the notion of potential mobility has been used for analysis. The basic premise here is those who are seriously dissatisfied with the overall housing situation will seek alternative accommodation or adapt their existing dwellings to their needs. Here we focus on those who intend to move, or are 'potentially mobile'. This may also reflect a greater degree of dissatisfaction than adaption. The approach then is to calibrate the thresholds for different housing attributes at which households decide to be potentially mobile. Since these thresholds are to be interpreted as housing preferences, it is also necessary to take account of certain socio-economic and demographic characteristics of households which may influence these preferences.

At an initial level, the households are distinguished as being potentially mobile (PM) and immobile. However, in this dual categorisation, the households who are extremely dissatisfied with their housing situation but are unable to consider a move, are clubbed with those who are actually satisfied with their housing. We have, therefore, divided the immobile households into those who are broadly satisfied (SI) with their housing situation and others, who are probably the constrained immobile households (CI). Empirically, this distinction was largely based on the reasons given by the households for not being potentially mobile. On the whole, for Ahmedabad, almost one-fourth of the households expressed a desire for change. Of the potentially immobile, only a little less than half were satisfied. Thus, almost 30 per cent of the households are constrained though potentially immobile.

TABLE 6.1
Extent of Potential Mobility

Mobility Status	Percentage of Total Households	
Potential Mobile (PM)	23.8	222
Potentially Immobile		
Constrained (CI)	28.8	268
Satisfied (SI)	47.4	442

Source: Primary survey.

The approach for this analysis is to distinguish amongst these three groups of households in terms of essentially two different sets of variables. The first refers to the household characteristics which may determine, both the housing preferences and constraints. Thus, household income on one hand may effect preferences or alternatively low levels of income may suggest severe constraints on housing expenditure and, therefore, the available housing opportunities. The next set of variables relates to housing attributes in terms of the current housing situation. Here the interpretation is mostly in terms of housing preferences. The variables used in the analysis and the results are presented in Tables A 6.1 to 6.3.

We may expect that the difference between potentially mobile and satisfied immobile (SET B) is more due to the differences in the housing situation. On the other hand, the potentially mobile and constrained immobile (SET A) are more likely to differ on household characteristics affecting constraints. Both the sets of variables, however, are likely to be important in distinguishing the satisfied and constrained immobile (SET C). Since the multi-dimensional housing product is essentially procured as a complete bundle of goods, to identify the relative preferences of households for different attributes of housing, it is necessary to adopt multivariate analysis. Multivariate regressions were run in three different

TABLE 6.2
Regression Sets for Multivariate Analysis

	Dependent Variable Description		Number of Observations
Set A	Potentially Mobile (PM)	= 0	490
	Constrained Immobile (CI)	= 1	
Set B	Potentially Mobile (PM)	= 0	664
	Satisfied Immobile (SI)	= 1	
Set C	Constrained Immobile (CI)	= 0	710
	Satisfied Immobile (SI)	= 1	

sets with the mobility status as a binary dependent variable as shown in Table 6.2.*

Housing Preferences

Given the analytical approach the housing preferences may be derived from the results of both SET B and SET C. The latter, however, may also indicate the constraints faced by the households. Since households choose on a large set of housing characteristics at the same time, the housing preferences are actually a process of trade-off. The main attributes on which these trade-offs probably take place are tenure, accessibility, size, shelter quality and neighbourhood quality. A detailed look has been attempted at each attribute in order to highlight the differing housing preferences and trade-offs by different groups of households.

TENURE

House ownership is probably one of the most important achievements for most households. Ownership gives a sense of security

* We are fully aware of the statistical problems associated with the assumptions of error term in using a dummy variable as a dependent variable for OLS estimation. Our discussion in subsequent sections only highlights the relative importance of explanatory variables. Mehta (1982) has shown, through comparison of OLS, Logit and Discriminant analysis, that for a dichotomous dependent variable, the OLS regressions

both in economic and psychological terms. Further, owning a house often also represents a major investment decision. As seen earlier, the rates of ownership in Ahmedabad are relatively higher than in the other metropolitan centres.

One of the important housing preferences is for tenure, or in other words, the desire to own a house. This is very clearly evident from the fact that compared to more than three-fourths of owner households amongst the SI group only a half or less were owners in the other two groups. Further, these differences were also statistically significant. Even in the regression results, this variable (OWND) remains consistently significant and stable. However, unlike the assumption of many recent housing policies, the legality of tenure does not seem to be a very high priority, as LEGTEN remains insignificant in the total sample.

Although the legality of tenure may not be very important, it would also not be correct to conclude that perception of tenure security is not important. The sample of hutment dwellers, where this may be important is small and therefore, it is difficult to assess. The earlier demand analysis showed that security of tenure affects demand positively at least for the owners. However, the effect is small as the sample was pooled. A large number of earlier descriptive studies both in Ahmedabad, and elsewhere in India and other developing countries have clearly shown the importance of tenure security for these groups (cf. Mehta, 1982a).

The importance of tenure remains unchanged even in equations with samples stratified by household incomes. OWND remained significant in both SET B and SET C for all income groups. However, its greater significance for the lower and upper-income groups, compared to the middle-income groups probably suggests some adjustment of aspiration regions by the middle-income group households. This may be due to the relatively restricted ownership housing opportunities for this group in the Ahmedabad housing market. This would be especially true for the kind of housing bundle sought by this group within their affordable budget in the ownership market. This is also reflected from the fact that EDUC is more important as a preference/constraint variable amongst the middle-income group households than even housing expenditure

provides similar order of importance of variables as the other methods and is thus a good enough first approximation despite the violation of assumptions of the error term.

(HSEXP2). This suggests that the housing preferences amongst the middle-income groups are affected to a great extent by the educational status. These high expectations are, however, not matched by the expenditure levels and available housing opportunities.

Another interesting observation for the income stratified results is the significance of LEGTEN for the middle and upper-income groups in SET C. This is also true for samples stratified by house type. However, here it is significant for the lower quality of houses. In both these cases, the coefficient is significant with a negative sign, suggesting that those with legal tenure are more likely to be constrained immobile (CI) groups. This is probably another case of adjusted aspirations due to an institutional factor like the Rent Control Act. Thus, the renters with legal tenure and with rent levels protected by institutional measures continue to be immobile, despite relatively high income and (probably) a changing housing priority structure. This is also borne out by earlier studies in chawls and pols where the rents are protected at extremely low levels due to the Rent Control Legislation. Thus, these households continue to stay in their current housing, despite significant housing dissatisfaction.

It may be postulated that with an increasing stage in the life cycle, the desire and probably the ability to own housing (due to a higher savings capacity) also increase. To analyse this, the samples were stratified by stages in the life cycle, with the expectation that the importance of ownership would be felt only in the second and third strata. Surprisingly, however, this does not seem to be true in Ahmedabad. Desire to own remains consistently high, except for the mature families in SET B. Not only is the OWND insignificant in this group, but its sign is negative suggesting that the owners are more likely to be potentially mobile. Further, unlike for other groups, the coefficient of legality of tenure (LEGTEN) is important and positive. This may be due to a group of owner households who lack tenure legality despite achieving higher income levels. This is supported by the fact that the average income for potentially mobile mature families is significantly higher than the satisfied immobile group. Thus, legality of tenure seems to become important with increasing incomes at later stages in the life cycle.

It is also likely that for different income groups, preferences, abilities and constraints at different stages in the life cycle, with respect to tenure are likely to vary in response to the market situation. A preliminary glance at the ownership rates by income

TABLE 6.3
Ownership by Income and Stage in Life Cycle

Household Income (Rupees per month)	Stage in Life Cycle			Total (No. of Observations)
	Young Family	Mature Family	Old Family	
700 or less	a. 0.54	0.55	0.56	0.55
	b. 0.53	0.55	0.61	0.56 (269)
701 to 1500	a. 0.49	0.63	0.50	0.54
	b. 0.61	0.80	0.75	0.72 (355)
1501 or more	a. 0.65	0.83	0.77	0.75
	b. 0.86	0.96	0.94	0.92 (308)

* Young family refers to those single or married households with children less than 10 years of age.
Mature families refer to married households with children between 10 and 20 years of age.
Old families refer to families with children above 20 years of age or old married couple staying alone.
a. Percentage of households who are owners.
b. Percentage of households whose tenure is legal.
Source: Primary survey.

and stage in the life cycle presents some interesting results. For the lowest income groups, there are only marginal and insignificant differences in ownership rates at different stages in the life cycle. This probably suggests not a lack of preference but a lack of savings and increase in demand with the stage in the life cycle. The ownership actually achieved is probably simply a reflection of different processes in the informal sector for gaining access to ownership. On the other hand, for the middle-income groups, the rates for mature families are a little higher but on the whole, significantly lower than for the upper-income groups. For the latter, the rates are high at all stages suggesting a relatively early entry in the ownership market.

For both the middle and upper-income groups, the ownership rates tend to taper off for the older families, though this is significant only for the middle-income groups. This may have two alternative explanations. Firstly, there may actually be a downward tenure mobility for the older families, so that the ownership house may be sold off for pecuniary benefits. Alternatively, and more plausibly, this is simply a reflection of the temporal changes in the market situation in terms of the available housing opportunities for this income group. When the old families were in their prime years in the fifties, the housing situation was probably quite tight, probably easing during the sixties when the currently mature families were looking for ownership housing.

ACCESSIBILITY TO WORK

Choice of a house is obviously linked to the choice of a location and the implied set of 'spatial relationships' with the urban system. It is quite likely that the journey to work is probably the most important of these relationships. As a matter of fact, many of the housing market models use a change in work location as the major motivating factor behind residential mobility.

Some differing viewpoints from these mainstream assumptions also exist. Stegman (1969), particularly questions the importance generally placed on work-home relationships. He advises that a more comprehensive view of location is important, considering the activity patterns as a whole for different members of the household rather than only the accessibility to work. In a rather different approach, Jones (1979), also indicates that 'locational factors are unimportant in the decision to move . . . . Accessibility is consistently found to be of only minor importance as a motivator in the mobility process'. On the other hand, amongst the more descriptive literature, the shelter location in relation to employment opportunities is identified as the highest priority, especially for the low income households at early stages in the life cycle in the developing countries (Turner, 1976 and Mehta, 1982a etc.).

From the above analysis, accessibility to work seems to be important only for the lower-income groups. This is clearly evident from the fact that TRVHEAD is insignificant throughout the entire analysis except when the sample is stratified by income. It then becomes significant only for the lowest income groups in both sets A and B. This clearly suggests the importance of work-home distance minimisation for those in the lower-income brackets, as seen in the significantly lesser time taken to travel to work for the lower-income groups. In fact, since a much greater proportion of workers in this group walk to work, the actual distance differences are probably much greater. It is also partly reflected from the fact that those in the eastern parts of Ahmedabad are more likely to work in the same or nearby zones as their zone of residence. On the other hand, the relatively higher-income groups on the western side often travel to the other side of the city. These differences, however, are also a reflection of the skewed distribution of economic activities in Ahmedabad.

TABLE 6.4
Travel for Work by Household Income

Household Income (Rupees per month)	Average Travel Time to Work (in minutes)		Predominant Modes Used
	Principal Worker	Secondary Earners	
Less than 700	13.8	14.6	Walk, Cycle, Mass Transport
701 to 1500	19.5	18.6	Cycle, Mass Transport
1501 or more	17.3	17.1	Own Vehicles Mass Transport

Source: Primary survey.

It is worth inquiring on the effect of residential location on the income earning opportunities and the levels of income actually achieved. Earlier studies of lower-income groups in Bangalore, Ahmedabad and Pune indicate that an inappropriate location can significantly affect the employment chances, especially for the secondary earners amongst the low-income groups (cf. Mehta, 1982a, and Swamy, 1983).

House Size

Most earlier literature report house size as the most important factor for potential mobility. It appears that in many western countries, 'dwelling size is the most widespread cause of housing dissatisfaction'. This is found to be true in Ahmedabad as well. More than 50 per cent of the potentially mobile households give inadequate space as the major reason for wanting to change residence. This proportion is significantly greater for those in lower quality house types, smaller houses, and at later stages in the life cycle. It is interesting, however, that there is no significant difference amongst different income groups in this regard. On the whole, the effect of house size on potential mobility seems important. This is brought out by the fact that, even for those households who do not give inadequate size as the major reason for mobility, the house size at 45.2 sq.m. is significantly lower than the 67 sq.m. for the satisfied households.

The housing preferences for size are also affected by the general availability of housing. Thus, in a dynamic perspective, in a generally improving situation, minimum levels would also increase as they have in western countries. However, in most developing countries, this has not been possible. Over the years, with an increasing awareness of the gap between housing costs and affordability, the planners' axe has generally fallen on the size of the house. In the early post-independence euphoria, it was common to find standards for minimum house sizes to be a little over 100 sq.m. Over the last few decades, in response to rapidly rising prices and dwindling resources allocated to housing, this standard has fallen rapidly. In the eighties it is common to find the 'acceptable minimum standards' to be about 20 to 30 sq.m. for a dwelling.

While discussing the house size, it is important to distinguish between this and house design, in terms of a division of the house in rooms. The latter is important in affording privacy to different members of the household. Further, our concern should be with the relationship between dwelling and household size, or the density of occupation. The most common indicator for this is the persons per room ratio (PPROOM). Our analysis presents some very interesting results regarding size preferences in this perspective. Along with tenure, house size is very clearly high on the preference list of most households. On the whole, for the total sample, both house size (HOUSESZ) and occupancy (PPROOM) are significant with the appropriate signs in SET B. However, when the sample is stratified by income, the results are quite different. For the lowest income groups, house size is more significant than PPROOM. This suggests that for these income groups it is much more important to give a flexible house with more area than an inflexible one with more rooms. However, for the upper-income groups, HOUSESZ is less relevant. The importance of appropriate number of rooms is evident from the highly significant PPROOM variable. These observations also hold when the sample is stratified by house type.

The effect of size becomes more complex in SET C which compares the constrained and satisfied immobile households. When the sample is stratified by income, only PPROOM is significant, especially for the middle-income groups. This may suggest that these households feel the available space to be inadequate especially as the household matures but are unable to find a 'better' house within their budget constraint. At the upper-income levels, they probably manage to increase the size of the house itself even though the overall structural quality may deteriorate. Thus, even the constrained immobile households overcome the size dissatisfaction due to other probable advantages of legal tenure, low rents and a favourable location if the incomes increase. This has major policy implications as the type of housing which affords later possibilities of increasing the house size becomes extremely important in satisfying this important need.

Besides the differences amongst households in different income groups regarding preference for size versus rooms. There are differences amongst households in terms of the size thresholds. On the whole, as seen in Table 6.5 it appears that some size increases are possible for all income groups as they advance in the life cycle stage. However, these increases are much more pronounced for the upper-income groups. It is only for these groups that the size increases are in relation to the increases in household size. In the two lower-income groups, the persons per room ratio also increases.

TABLE 6.5
House Size by Household Income and Stage in Life Cycle

Household Income (Rupees per month)	Stage in Life Cycle			Total
	Young Family	Mature Family	Old Family	
Less than 700	a. 29.7	51.9	28.1	35.5
	b. 1.77	1.44	1.93	1.72
	c. 3.8	1.9	3.4	4.0
701 to 1500	a. 30.8	36.9	47.3	38.3
	b. 1.89	2.14	2.35	2.12
	c. 3.2	3.6	3.7	3.5
1501 or more	a. 52.4	72:7	106.3	83.3
	b. 2.85	3.76	4.10	3.68
	c. 3.4	2.2	2.3	2.5

Note: a. Mean house size in sq.m.
b. Mean number of rooms.
c. Mean ratio of persons per room.

The effect of house size on potential mobility status seems clearly linked to the size of the household also. There are clear variations amongst different income groups in terms of the satisfaction thresholds for house size. The average house size of the potentially mobile households in the three income groups is 25.7, 34.6 and 59.6 sq.m. respectively. The sizes which are satisfactory are, however, much higher, ranging from 38.6 to 102.4 sq.m. On the other hand, there are no significant differences amongst different income groups in terms of thresholds for persons per room for potential mobility. Thus, this range is narrow from 4.0 to 4.2 only.

These discussions suggest that it is possible to identify the threshold ranges for aspiration region for house size for different income groups. Clearly, these are not based on only need but also influenced by the perception of affordability and housing opportunities and the relative importance of the house size. These are probably between 30 to 50 sq.m. for the lowest-income groups and become higher for the upper-income groups as shown in Table 6.7. These also correspond well with the house size sought by the potentially mobile for both the lower and upper-income groups. The middle-income groups, once again appear to have much greater expectations compared to actual situations.

These observations suggest that one should be wary of programmes which drastically reduce even the plot sizes for lower-income groups below these thresholds on the grounds of affordability. Analysis of housing by income groups suggest that overall land requirements are not very sensitive to the size changes at the lower end of the income spectrum in any case (Mehta et al., 1986). Secondly, it is very important to evolve designs which afford size increases at later stages in an easy and efficient manner.

Shelter Quality

Till recently, most housing policies in India emphasised the shelter quality, mainly in terms of the materials used. However, it is gradually being recognised that the quality of housing may include much more than this. A major shift which has occurred is in terms of the need to look at the quality of utilities or infrastructure. The two main programmes of sites and services and environmental improvement are thus oriented to this latter aspect.

The most obvious variable to capture a variety of quality factors might have been the house type. However, the dummy variables

TABLE 6.6

House Size by Stage in Life Cycle, Household Income and Mobility Status

		Stage in Life Cycle			Household Income			Total
		Young	*Mature*	*Old*	*0 to 700*	*701 to 1500*	*1.500 or more*	
Potentially Mobile	a.	31.0	42.7	47.4	25.7	34.6	59.6	39.6
	b.	1.81	2.28	1.95	1.53	1.81	2.72	2.00
	c.	4.37	3.70	4.56	4.21	4.39	4.01	4.22
Satisfied Immobile	a.	47.7	51.8	91.5	38.6	45.7	102.4	67.0
	b.	2.62	3.04	3.80	2.21	2.61	4.36	3.22
	c.	2.67	2.23	2.18	3.32	2.60	1.54	2.35
Constrained Immobile	a.	23.1	59.0	37.5	38.6	31.3	52.5	38.6
	b.	1.58	1.77	2.19	1.26	1.73	2.78	1.80
	c.	3.90	5.03	3.64	4.66	3.99	3.90	4.20

Note: a. Mean house size in sq.m.
b. Mean number of rooms.
c. Mean ratio of persons per room.

Source: Primary survey.

TABLE 6.7
Thresholds for Housing Size by Income Groups

	Household Income (Rupees per month)		
	Less than 700	701 to 1500	1501 or more
Below which at least 75 per cent will be potentially mobile	30	46	71
Above which at least 25 per cent will be satisfied immobile	50.0	56.8	106.1
Mean house size sought by potentially mobile households (sq.m.)	46.7	70.4	97.9
Mean house size (per capita) sought by potentially mobile households (sq.m.)	9.8	11.6	14.9

Source: Primary survey.

for house types proved to be not very important, partly because they also bear close relationship with income and some of the other variables. We have, therefore, used two indices to reflect different aspects of shelter quality. Structural Quality (STRUQ) essentially reflects the materials used for walls and roof and the observed structural condition. The second variable is an index developed on the basis of the quality of utilities like water supply, toilets, and electricity. Another variable (SURFQ), an index based on the finishing of walls, floors and fixtures failed to give any meaningful results. This may suggest that most households give less importance to appearance and more to the structural quality. It was, however, significant and positive for renters and those in the lower house type.

Whether due to the demonstration effect of the past policies or otherwise, STRUQ is a very significant variable throughout the analysis. In this respect it seems as important as tenure for most households. There is some difference amongst different groups, however. It is not significant for the lower income households for whom work-home relationship for the head was more important. For the same income group, however, STRUQ is important in SET C, probably suggesting more of a constraint than preference.

Thus, those in the lower structural quality are likely to be constrained immobile, having adjusted their aspirations due to a lack of housing opportunity.

The utility variable becomes significant for some groups in SET C, especially middle-income groups; for huts, chawls and pols dwellers; and for renters at a later stage in the life cycle. This is also a very clear case of adjusted aspiration levels. It is important to note that for the lower house type and renters, STRUQ is not significant. Thus UTILQ is simply a proxy variable in this case. In the lower house type (especially 'slum' settlements), provision of utilities generally implies security of tenure. Thus, the significance of UTILQ probably reflects the importance of tenure security.

Most housing analysts use the age of dwelling as a proxy for shelter quality whereby the older buildings would imply lower shelter quality. Our analysis, however, suggests a reverse of this. With greater value of DWAGE, a given household is more likely to be satisfied immobile. DWAGE is significant for upper-income groups, young households, owners and those in lower house type. The results for the hutments and chawls may reflect the process of upgradation. Thus, the older the dwelling, more likely it is to be of better quality. The significance of DWAGE for the owners also suggests the same reasoning. This is very similar to Jimminez's (1982) findings for a low income settlement in Indonesia.

Neighbourhood Quality

Theoretically, it may be expected that the quality of neighbourhood is an important dimension of housing preferences. This was also reflected in stated attributes for the best and worst part of the current housing situation where both physical and social environment appear to be important. In the multivariate regression analysis, however, a number of variables reflecting the physical and social qualities of the neighbourhood were found to be insignificant in the preliminary analysis. This was largely on account of smaller variations in the sample observation.

We would, thus, refrain from concluding that neighbourhood quality is not as important as the social and physical environment of the neighbourhood; good access to facilities clearly emerges from the stated preferences through direct questioning on the best aspects of the current housing environment. Almost one-third of the households felt that an appropriate social environment was the best aspect of their current house. This was much higher for the lower-income groups. On the whole, the importance of neighbourhood seems to be greater for the lower-income groups. It is also likely that most people manage to stay in areas which have good social access for them. This may be due to the fact that social networks are used to locate housing.

TABLE 6.8
Best Aspects of the Current Housing Situation

Attributes	Household Income (Rupees per month)			Total
	Less than 700	701 to 1500	1501 or more	
Social Environment	42.2	27.0	23.0	30.1
Physical Environment	11.2	13.4	16.2	13.7
Facilities	22.1	23.7	18.2	21.4
Shelter Quality	16.7	25.5	29.4	24.1
House Size	4.7	4.3	8.8	5.9
Access to Work	3.1	6.1	4.4	4.8
Total	100.0	100.0	100.0	100.0

Source: Primary survey.

Constraints in Housing Behaviour

As postulated earlier, households may be greatly constrained in their residential behaviour. This affects the level and nature of the trade-offs that they have to make. The most important amongst these is likely to be the usually recognised budget constraint. The ability and willingness to spend on housing and the possibility of getting financial assistance for housing may pose formidable constraints. Similarly, another important aspect may be the information constraint. This relates to both the awareness and the accuracy of the information. Besides these, there may be other constraints which arise out of the market and institutional context prevailing in the given housing market. The market conditions may be in terms of the available housing opportunities and the prevailing prices. The institutional context refers to the presence of specific legislation like the Rent Control Act.

ECONOMIC CONSTRAINTS

In order to ascertain the influence of the economic constraints, both the monthly household income and the imputed monthly housing expenditure were included. The latter is a comprehensive measure including both the current out-of-pocket expenditure on housing like rent, repayment for housing loan, usual maintenance and repairs and property taxes, as well as the opportunity costs of paid up capital. The latter includes both the down payments or price paid for owners and any 'pugree' or deposits, for tenants. The opportunity cost of this capital is taken at 1 per cent per month.

The influence of income and housing demand on actual residential behaviour may be very complex. It has already been noted that income class affects preferences. At the same time, the potential mobility status may also be affected to a great extent by the economic factors. Our earlier findings suggested low income elasticities of demand which is partly due to the fact that there are many other factors which affect the actual housing expenditure. These include housing circumstances and the market situation faced in terms of the available housing opportunities, rather than only demographic factors like stage in the life cycle. For the total sample, INCOME is negative and significant only in SET B highlighting its effect on housing preferences.

The other major preference variable appears to be the education level of the head of household wherein higher income and educational levels increase housing expectations—making households potentially more mobile. On the other hand, HSEXP2 is positive and significant in SET C, as it is the main constraining variable. Thus only with higher housing expenditure levels is it possible to achieve satisfactory housing conditions. Surprisingly, a relatively greater housing expenditure is more necessary in lower house type where HSEXP2 is highly significant. The only puzzling result is for renters where both INCOME and HSEXP2 are negative and significant in SET C This probably suggests that there is a group of tenants who despite having a high level of housing expenditure, are unable to attain better housing and therefore feel quite constrained.

To get a more detailed understanding of these aspects, the differences in housing expenditure patterns for different groups by income and stage in life cycle groups was studied (Table 6.9). One

TABLE 6.9

Housing Expenditure by Stage in Life Cycle, Household Income and Potential Mobility Status

	Potential Mobility Status								
	Potentially Mobile			Satisfied Immobile			Constrained Immobile		
	a	b	(b ÷ a)	a	b	(b ÷ a)	a	b	(b ÷ a)
Stage in Life Cycle									
Young	96.6	131.3	1.35	143.5	325.0	2.27	80.7	108.6	1.34
Mature	121.7	257.2	2.11	144.8	339.3	2.34	69.1	107.6	1.55
Old	108.9	169.1	1.55	117.6	346.6	2.96	80.3	128.7	1.60
Household Income									
Less than 700	58.0	81.1	1.39	68.2	210.9	3.09	67.5	74.3	1.10
701 to 1500	128.5	185.9	1.45	114.9	261.0	2.27	81.9	142.8	1.74
1501 or more	130.7	277.5	2.12	188.0	479.8	2.55	81.2	117.3	1.44
Total	108.3	182.8	1.69	132.9	337.7	2.54	76.8	113.6	1.48

Source: Primary survey.
a = Actual output of packet housing expenditure—Rupees per month.
b = Housing expenditure, including opportunity cost of paid-up capital.

of the important observations is related to the higher HSEXP2 compared to the actual out-of-pocket housing expenditure (HSEXP1) for the satisfied immobile group. This remains true even across the various stages in the life cycle and income groups. The differential is much greater however, for the lower-income groups suggesting that in this group, the satisfied immobile are the few lucky ones who have managed to get access to finance. It is clear from this analysis that a major difference between the satisfied immobile and the other potentially mobile and constrained immobile groups, is the ability to invest in housing.

An analysis of perceived affordability of the potentially mobile household indicates that the middle-income households are willing to back up their higher housing expectations by showing greater propensity to spend on it. However, even this is not adequate in relation to the prevailing market prices as the ratio of estimated market price of a desired house to the affordable cost is as high as 4.2. Further, in reality there are not many avenues of assistance for housing finance open to this group. Most of the private sector efforts in Ahmedabad so far have catered to upper-income groups. Surprisingly, even the low-income groups are willing to spend as much as 25 per cent of their income on housing of their own choice. However, their probable lower levels of savings are reflected in a much lower down payment potential. The market price of their desired housing is well beyond their means even if financial assistance was available. The effect of these realities, however, simply forces the lower-income groups into the informal sector where they are increasingly at the mercy of slumlords. The middle-income groups, on the other hand, become constrained adjustors or even downwardly mobile in terms of their housing situation.

INSTITUTIONAL CONSTRAINTS

Besides the obvious economic constraints which are compounded by the disparities in financial assistance for housing, there may be other institutional factors which also constrain household behaviour. A good case in point is the Rent Control Legislation. Whatever may be its effects on housing supply, it has certainly been one of the major factors inhibiting residential mobility in Ahmedabad housing market.

Theoretically, a household would seek housing adjustments if there was a significant mismatch between the adjusted aspiration

TABLE 6.10
Perception of Affordability of Potentially Mobile Households

Affordability Criteria	Household Income (Rupees per month)			Total
	Less than 700	701 to 1500	More than 1501	
● Affordable monthly expenditure on housing	118.5	214.4	473.1	254.9
● Affordable monthly expenditure as a percent of household income	24.9	20.8	12.2	19.6
● Affordable expenditure as a multiple of current housing expenditure				
Actual-HSEXP1	5.7	7.8	15.9	9.4
Imputed-HSEXP2	4.2	6.0	6.5	5.6
● Affordable down payment (Rupees)	4977	17364	20661	15014
● Down payment as a multiple of monthly household income	11.6	14.0	7.1	11.5
● Estimated total affordable cost using HUDCO's terms of finance for different income groups*	21204	34774	57707	36931
● Estimated loan as a multiple of expected loan	4.14	2.17	1.37	2.48
● Estimated market price** of desired house as a multiple of estimated affordable cost	4.4	4.2	2.8	3.9
● Responding households	41	61	46	148

* The estimated cost does not take into consideration the ceiling costs imposed by HUDCO. The revised HUDCO norms as per 1986 are used.
** Market price is estimated using hedonic function results for the characteristics of desired house. See Note for Table 6.11.

regions (or housing preferences) and the current housing situation. However, this decision also involves a comparison of housing costs. Thus, as postulated earlier, a household will contemplate change only if the difference in utility from a perceived affordable opportunity and current housing situation exceeds the transaction costs and differentials in housing expenditure.

In the rent control situation, since the renter household is paying a very low and fixed price, the expenditure differential between the two situations is always very high and is increasing. Further, continued stay in the neighbourhood adversely affects the propensity to move as one develops stronger ties with the area. Therefore, the utility gap between a potential new opportunity and current situation narrows further. It is then likely that households in such a situation, though not satisfied with the housing situation, do not consider mobility. Our results indicate that amongst the renters in the formal sector, those with legal status who receive rent receipts are more likely to be immobile and less likely to even contemplate mobility. The constrained immobility of the renters in the informal sector, however, is more indicative of the increasing difficulties faced by the renters in this sector and the loss of popular control over their own housing.

Some further interesting and collaborating evidence also emerges from the regression analysis in terms of the influence of the legality of tenure (LEGTEN). This is significant and negative for certain groups in SET C and positive and significant for certain groups in SET A. In SET C, LEGTEN is important in samples stratified by house type and for middle and upper-income groups. Thus, though the effect of rent control is important in all the house types, its protection probably accrues much more to the middle and upper-income groups. The differential impact on income groups is also brought out from the results of SET C. For the upper-income groups and for the other house type category, LEGTEN significantly contributes to the probability of a household being constrained immobile. This is also true for the renters when the sample is stratified by tenure and for mature households in samples stratified by stages in the life cycle. Thus, renters with legal tenure, at mature stage and with higher level of income are constrained immobile.

The implication that emerges from this analysis is that the true housing demand is not reflected in the market because of certain institutional factors. Further, these imbalances seem to favour the relatively better off sections of population. This is partially reflected from the expenditure pattern of renters. The constrained immobile renters, especially those at advancing stages in the life cycle spend significantly lesser amounts than both the satisfied and potentially mobile renters. For those in the early stages, there is no difference between the potentially mobile and constrained immobile. However, the satisfied renters in this group, pay very high rents. This is another indirect effect of Rent Control Act in which the relatively recent entrants end up paying higher rental prices.

HOUSING INFORMATION AND AWARENESS

Imperfection in the housing market is likely to be due to the extremely weak information base. Most households in our sample use only social contacts to gain information of housing opportunities. Even in cases of past mobility, the moves were almost always supported by information based on 'friends and relatives'.

The degree of awareness of the housing market is difficult to assess. Our approach has been to analyse this on the basis of the responses of potentially mobile households regarding their housing search. Admittedly, this has reduced the sample size considerably. We attempted to understand the type of house that the potentially mobile households are looking for and their perceived affordability and market prices for such a house. These were then compared with the market prices of similar houses estimated on the basis of the hedonic functions developed in the previous chapters.

First of all, awareness and expectations of institutional finance is rather low for the entire sample, though there were clear variations in the anticipated source of finance for housing amongst the potentially mobile in different income groups. The middle and upper-income groups seemed to base their expectations on their accumulated savings with employers or loans. On the other hand, low-income households expected assistance from informal sources such as relatives and friends. On the whole only about one-fifth of the households cite institutional finance as a potential source of finance for home ownership. The important constraint probably relates to a lack of adequate opportunity to avail institutional finance. As seen earlier, the role of the public sector, with which the bulk of institutional funding is linked, is rather limited. The other source of institutional finance from the cooperative society has, in the past, accrued largely to the upper-income groups.

It is also important to ascertain the accuracy of the information which the potentially mobile households actually seem to possess. One of the crucial variables is the perceived market price of the

TABLE 6.11
Realities of Perceived Market Price

Ratio of Hedonic* Function Based on Market Price to Perceived Price	Household Income (Rupees per month)			Total
	Less than 700	701 to 1500	More than 1500	
1.0 or less	14.6	11.5	21.7	15.6
1.1 to 1.5	12.3	22.9	21.7	19.6
1.6 to 2.0	24.4	32.8	37.0	31.7
2.1 to 3.0	21.9	24.6	6.6	18.2
3.1 or more	26.8	8.2	13.0	14.9
Responding households	100.0	100.0	100.0	100.0
	(41)	(61)	(46)	(148)
Average	2.41	1.87	1.71	1.97

* This price was estimated by using results of hedonic functions to the characteristics of houses which the potentially mobile sought in the market. The characteristics used are location, size, house type and tenure.

type of house which they seek in the market. The results of hedonic functions developed in the previous chapter were applied to the housing characteristics sought by the potentially mobile. It appears that very few households (15.5 per cent) had a reasonable assessment of the market price. On the whole, the lower income households underestimated the market price nearly 2.5 times as against 1.8 and 1.7 for the middle and higher income households.

This apparent lack of understanding of the housing market operation stems from the weak information base about housing at the city level. Except for newspaper advertisements, individuals in the city have to rely on their personal contacts to ascertain availability of housing. Information on land or home prices are just not available to the consumers and they have to either search the market or believe the offer price of new housing as the market price.

Summary

The analysis in this chapter suggests that preferences are affected to a great extent by the prevailing market conditions and perceptions of opportunities and awareness. It is clear that the effects of restrictive situations are either to constrain the households or to force them to adjust their aspirations. The differences are most pronounced in relation to tenures. It appears that preference for ownership is important for all households though to a certain extent, it does become more pronounced at later stages in the life cycle. Legality of tenure, on the other hand, is not a high priority though it also becomes important at later stages in the life cycle, if higher incomes are attained. Interestingly, the continuing preference for legal tenure, especially by the middle income groups, despite opportunity constraints in the ownership market seem to be affected by the higher level of educational attainment amongst these groups.

Distinct variations exist amongst the different income groups in terms of what is actually achieved. A large proportion of the lower-income groups, attain ownership though 'informal' processes where the stage in the life cycle does not seem to have any influence. For the middle-income groups, however, the situation is tight since the preferences are more towards legal tenure and a certain level of house quality but within context of limited opportunities. It is only for the relatively upper-income groups that high rates of ownership are actually possible.

The low priority of lower-income groups for legal tenure probably reflects a trade-off against the need for high accessibility to work. Inappropriate residential location can significantly affect employment chances, especially for the secondary earners. Earlier studies in Ahmedabad and Bangalore have indicated that even the earning levels for the same type of occupations are greatly affected by residential location, e.g., Mehta (1982), Swamy (1984).

House size, though important for all levels, shows some interesting variations. The lower-income groups seem to be concerned more about the overall area of the house whereas the preference of upper-income groups is more towards size in terms of number of rooms. On the whole, all income groups manage some size increases as they advance in the life cycle stage, however, these are much more pronounced for the upper-income groups.

The inability of most households to significantly improve the occupancy rate in relation to low levels of residential mobility suggests a need for housing which has provision for upgradation in later stages and an increase in house size. The greater expectations of middle-income strata in relation to opportunities and actual achievements are also reflected in size thresholds where the expectations are well beyond the actual ranges achieved by them in Ahmedabad. Even for the lower-income groups, the thresholds and achievements are well above the 20 to 25 sq.m. houses which seem to be commonly acceptable as the minimum sizes in many public sector projects.

Although shelter quality is important for the middle and upper-income groups, the lower-income strata probably trade this off against work accessibility and social access which are more important for them. The possibility of progressive upgradation seems very important in huts and chawls and amongst owners as suggested by a preference for older dwellings.

In terms of economic factors, it appears that the level of household income affects housing preferences along with the educational attainment of the head of the household. A very crucial influence, however, is the question of access to housing finance. Besides the economic constraints in relation to housing and finance opportunities, institutional factors like rent control legislation also affect residential behaviour.

On the whole, then, the picture that emerges from the Ahmedabad housing market is of a very imbalanced distribution of opportunities. The effect on the lower-income groups especially is to completely adjust their aspiration levels and to be forced to trade-off both shelter quality and tenure legality. These adjusted aspirations make their preferences appear quite distinct from the others. On the other hand, the middle-income groups have not adjusted their aspirations to a great extent. They are, therefore, much more likely to be potentially mobile. Only those who manage to gain access to either public housing or housing finance are able to achieve their aspirations generally at later stages in the life cycle. Their expectations, however, continue to be above what they can actually achieve in the market. Further, only the relatively high income groups are able to achieve satisfactory housing easily and early in the life cycle.

TABLE A6.1
Variables for Regression Analysis

Variable Description	Variable Name
1. Total household income from all sources (Rupees per month)	INCOME
2. Total housing expenditure-inclusive of opportunity cost of paid up capital (Price/Pugree) Rupees per month)	HSEXP2
3. Household size	HHSIZE
4. Stage in life cycle of head of household	STLIFE
1 Single person or unmarried	
2 Young married couple with no children	
3 Married couple with children—eldest child less than 10 years of age	
4 Mature families-married couple with the eldest child between 10 and 20 years of age	
5 Married couples with children above 20 but unmarried	
6 Married head with married children	
7 Old married staying alone or in extended households	
5. Education of head of household in terms of years completed	YRSEDUC
6. Mobility rate- number of moves made in the local market divided by the duration in the local housing market	MOBRATE
7. Dummy for ownership status (if self Owned = 1, otherwise = 0)	OWND
8. Dummy for legality of tenure (if tenure, status is legal (for owners, freehold ownership with the necessary permissions and for renters, rent receipt) = 1, otherwise 0)	LEGTEN
9. Built-up area of the dwelling unit in sq.mts.	HOUSESZ
10. Persons per room ratio	PRPROOM
11. Age of dwelling in years	DWAGE
12. The structural quality of dwelling (Scores developed out of wall and roof quality and structural condition)	STRQ
13. The surface quality of dwelling (Scores developed out of exterior conditions of walls finishing, flooring and openings)	SURFQ
14. Quality of utilities in or for the dwelling (Scores developed out of level and quality of water supply, drainage and toilets)	UTILQ
15. Travel time to work for the head of household (daily in minutes)	TRTMHD
16. Dummy for location in the walled city	WALLD
17. Dummy for location in upper-income areas	UPINCD

Note: To identify the intra-group differences, analysis was also carried out for samples stratified by income, stage in life cycle, house type and current tenure.

TABLE A6.2
Means and Standard Deviations for Variables for Regression Analysis

Variable	Means and Standard Deviation		
	Set A	*Set B*	*Set C*
INCOME	1565.75	1698.38	1339.89
	(1477.10)	(1613.13)	(1226.13)
HSEXP2	253.13	285.94	144.97
	(434.75)	(445.27)	(210.91)
HHSIZE	6.11	6.12	6.36
	(4.04)	(3.96)	(6.12)
STLIFE	4.09	4.17	3.91
	(1.49)	(1.53)	(1.37)
YRSEDUC	8.57	9.31	8.65
	(7.65)	(8.26)	(10.30)
MOBRATE	4.79	4.14	6.29
	(13.36)	(7.46)	(15.53)
OWND	0.64	0.68	0.46
LEGTEN	0.76	0.77	0.67
HOUSESZ	56.30	57.88	39.06
	(75.51)	(66.55)	(61.98)
PRPROOM	3.05	2.97	4.21
	(2.79)	(2.86)	(2.80)
DWAGE	54.71	48.57	45.68
	(145.61)	(126.16)	(100.52)
STRQ	9.61	9.70	8.83
	(1.72)	(1.61)	(1.81)
SURFQ	9.46	9.60	8.78
	(2.15)	(2.03)	(2.26)
UTILQ	6.04	6.17	5.51
	(2.33)	(2.24)	(2.39)
TRTMHD	17.10	17.99	16.00
	(18.99)	(18.18)	(18.43)
WALLD	0.13	0.11	0.16
UPINCD	0.32	0.36	0.20
Dependent Variable	0.62	0.67	0.55
	(0.49)	(0.47)	(0.50)
Sample size	(N = 710)	(N = 664)	(N = 490)

TABLE A6.3a

Determinants of Potential Mobility Status—SET A
DEPENDENT VARIABLE: MOBILITY STATUS
POT. MOBILE = 0, CONSTRAINED IMMOBILE = 1

Variable Name	Total Samples		House Type			Tenure			
			Huts, Chawls, Pols		Others		Renter		Owner
INCOME	-0.000048	(2.16)	-0.00007	(2.03)	0.000007	(0.24)	-0.00005	(1.05)	-0.00003	(0.97)
HSEXP2	-0.000304	(2.43)	-0.0002	(0.72)	-0.0002	(1.13)	-0.0004	(1.79)	-0.0002	(1.13)
HHSIZE	0.0095	(0.83)	0.01	(0.78)	-0.008	(0.36)	0.012	(0.68)	0.009	(0.61)
STLIFE	-0.0249	(1.45)	-0.01	(0.71)	-0.08	(2.52)	-0.04	(1.54)	-0.03	(1.33)
YRSEDUC	-0.00513	(2.19)	-0.003	(0.104)	-0.03	(2.95)	-0.004		-0.01	
MOBRATE	0.00212	(1.37)	0.002	(1.35)	-0.11	(0.20)	0.003	(1.54)	0.008	(1.97)
OWND	-0.0475	(1.01)	0.03	(0.56)	-0.25	(2.52)	—		—	
LEGTEN	0.0674	(1.17)	0.06	(0.50)	0.36	(2.55)	0.45	(2.07)	0.07	(0.63)
HOUSESZ	0.00015	(0.39)	0.0003	(0.74)	-0.52	(0.45)	0.0006	(1.55)	-0.001	(1.12)
PRPROOM	-0.0179	(1.46)	-0.02	(1.69)	0.44	(0.11)	-0.02	(1.45)	-0.02	(0.93)
DWAGE	0.00033	(1.44)	0.0003	(1.20)	0.39	(1.09)	0.0005	(1.55)	0.0003	(0.89)

Table A6.3a contd.

Variable Name	Total Samples		House Type			Tenure		
			Huts, Chawls, Pols		Others		Renter	Owner
STRUQ	0.0139	(0.46)	-0.01	(0.69)	0.16	(0.43)	0.02 (0.96)	-0.048 (1.91)
SURFQ	-0.0073	(0.46)	-0.01	(0.69)	0.16	(0.43)	0.02 (0.96)	-0.048 (1.91)
UTILQ	0.00307	(0.30)	0.003	(0.33)	0.21	(0.88)	0.02 (1.41)	0.004 (0.25)
TRTMHD	-0.0006	(0.48)	-0.0009	(0.62)	-0.25	(0.10)	0.0006 (0.36)	-0.002 (1.07)
WALLD	0.0249	(0.36)	—		—		0.03 (0.31)	0.096 (0.76)
UPINCD	-0.065	(1.06)	—		—		-0.05 (0.51)	-0.08 (0.96)
INTERCEPT	0.6945		0.57		0.79		0.372	0.894
R-SQUARE	0.073		0.051		0.21		0.09	0.15
F-RATIO	2.20		1.14		2.52		1.59	2.32
N	490		330		160		261	229

Note: Figures in parenthesis are 't' values.

TABLE A6.3b

Variable Name	Income			Stage in Life Cycle		
	0 to 700	701 to 1500	1501 or more	Young	Mature	Old
INCOME	—	—	—	0.00002 (0.47)	-0.00005 (1.56)	-0.00001 (0.30)
HSEXP2	-0.0003 (0.692)	-0.00007 (0.437)	-0.0007 (3.29)	-0.0004 (1.49)	-0.0004 (1.67)	0.000004 (0.02)
HHSIZE	-0.024 (0.71)	0.012 (0.613)	0.007 (0.47)	-0.038 (1.81)	0.05 (30.7)	-0.007 (0.29)
STLIFE	-0.039 (1.15)	-0.005 (0.18)	-0.03 (0.87)	—	—	—
YRSEDUC	0.001 (0.29)	-0.011 (3.65)	-0.009 (0.97)	0.002 (0.59)	-0.008 (2.31)	-0.01 (1.41)
MOBRATE	0.003 (1.58)	0.006 (1.32)	-0.003 (0.54)	0.003 (1.70)	0.006 (1.14)	-0.006 (0.79)
OWND	-0.034 (0.39)	0.057 (0.79)	-0.246 (2.48)	-0.004 (0.05)	-0.09 (1.13)	-0.06 (0.71)
LEGTEN	0.109 (0.97)	-0.010 (0.12)	0.248 (1.71)	0.07 (0.77)	0.22 (2.09)	0.02 (0.12)
HOUSESZ	0.0005 (1.18)	-0.001 (1.13)	0.151 (0.15)	-0.004 (2.47)	0.0003 (0.74)	-0.001 (1.22)
PRPROOM	0.057 (1.85)	-0.028 (1.46)	-0.381 (1.95)	-0.002 (0.07)	-0.025 (1.24)	-0.025 (0.99)
DWAGE	0.0004 (0.78)	0.0002 (0.61)	0.646 (1.74)	0.0003 (0.63)	0.0007 (1.92)	0.00005 (0.14)
STRUQ	-0.04 (1.17)	0.084 (2.97)	-0.285 (0.63)	-0.02 (0.74)	-0.006 (0.18)	0.03 (0.82)
SURFO	0.01 (0.43)	-0.058 (2.27)	0.354 (0.84)	0.025 (0.96)	-0.03 (0.09)	0.003 (0.11)
UTILO	0.02 (1.01)	0.0004 (0.03)	0.172 (0.71)	0.036 (2.28)	-0.02 (1.07)	-0.03 (1.49)
TRTMHD	0.004 (1.66)	-0.001 (0.57)	-0.003 (1.17)	-0.0006 (0.35)	-0.001 (0.45)	-0.00007 (0.02)
WALLD	0.108 (0.79)	0.233 (1.98)	-0.321 (2.54)	-0.14 (1.26)	-0.145 (1.21)	0.34 (2.23)
UPINCD	0.047 (0.39)	-0.198 (2.15)	-0.075 (0.66)	-0.04 (0.43)	-0.01 (0.09)	-0.04 (0.26)
INTERCEPT	0.559	0.53	0.72	0.65	0.83	0.77
R-SQUARE	0.109	0.176	0.27	0.12	0.27	0.15
F-RATIO	1.08	2.50	2.61	1.59	3.35	1.35
N	158	204	248	195	158	137

Note: Figures in parenthesis are 't' values.

TABLE A6.4a
Determinants of Potential Mobility Status—SET B
DEPENDENT VARIABLE: MOBILITY STATUS

POT. MOBILE = 0, STATISFIED IMMOBILE = 1

Variable Name	Total Samples		House Type		Tenure	
			Huts, Chawls, Pols	Others	Renter	Owner
INCOME	-0.000037	(2.95)	-0.00008 (2.68)	-0.00002 (1.34)	-0.001 (2.72)	-0.00002 (1.36)
HSEXP2	0.00003	(0.80)	0.0003 (1.87)	0.00005 (1.22)	0.00004 (0.25)	-0.00004 (0.96)
HHSIZE	0.01005	(1.71)	-0.001 (0.08)	0.03 (3.76)	0.02 (0.97)	0.008 (1.37)
STLIFE	-0.0035	(0.31)	0.01 (0.71)	-0.02 (1.28)	-0.03 (1.39)	0.001 (0.08)
YRSEDUC	-0.0063	(2.86)	-0.005 (1.71)	-0.009 (2.49)	-0.003 (0.96)	-0.013 (3.03)
MOBRATE	-0.0056	(2.40)	-0.005 (1.20)	-0.0006 (0.21)	-0.007 (2.31)	-0.001 (0.35)
OWND	0.117	(2.94)	0.21 (3.82)	-0.1 (1.55)	—	—
LEGTEN	-0.0209	(0.44)	-0.05 (0.84)	0.14 (1.40)	0.03 (0.38)	-0.04 (0.61)
HOUSESZ	0.0006	(0.91)	0.0008 (1.14)	0.0003 (0.97)	0.001 (1.25)	0.0005 (1.76)
PRPROOM	-0.0339	(3.49)	-0.02 (1.44)	-0.10 (4.49)	-0.04 (2.12)	-0.03 (2.58)
DWAGE	0.00037	(2.63)	0.0002 (1.32)	0.0007 (0.54)	0.0005 (1.41)	0.0003 (2.22)

Table A6.4a contd.

Variable Name	Total Samples		House Type				Tenure			
			Huts, Chawls, Pols		Others		Renter		Owner	
STRUQ	0.077	(5.48)	0.06	(2.79)	0.09	(2.93)	0.06	(2.47)	0.08	(4.60)
SURFQ	-0.0025	(0.21)	0.01	(0.76)	-0.01	(0.61)	0.05	(2.41)	-0.036	(1.78)
UTILQ	0.007	(0.82)	0.02	(1.36)	-0.006	(0.56)	0.008	(0.61)	0.009	(0.83)
TRTMHD	0.00024	(0.26)	0.0003	(0.18)	0.001	(1.09)	0.001	(0.79)	-0.0002	(0.19)
WALLD	-0.134	(2.14)	—		—		-0.2	(1.75)	-0.09	(1.27)
UPINCD	0.0558	(1.38)	—		—		0.025	(0.30)	0.09	(1.95)
INTERCEPT	-0.0460		-0.23		0.0037		-0.346		0.218	
R-SQUARE	0.23		0.24		0.16		0.30		0.16	
F-RATIO	11.5		5.82		4.54		5.16		5.32	
N	664		285		379		210		454	

Note: Figures in parenthesis are 't' values.

TABLE A6.4b
Determinants of Potential Mobility Status—SET B
DEPENDENT VARIABLE: MOBILITY STATUS

POT. MOBILE = 0, STATISFIED IMMOBILE = 1

Variable Name	Income						Stage in Life Cycle					
	0 to 700		701 to 1500		1501 or more		Young		Mature		Old	
INCOME	—		—		—		-0.00004	(1.53)	-0.00007	(2.64)	-0.00002	(0.90)
HSEXP2	-0.000001	(0.03)	-0.00001	(0.11)	0.00005	(0.88)	0.00006	(1.00)	0.00003	(0.27)	0.00004	(0.57)
HHSIZE	0.0044	(0.45)	0.018	(0.35)	0.0008	(0.07)	0.005	(0.68)	0.02	(1.17)	0.007	(0.76)
STLIFE	-0.009	(0.44)	0.004	(0.15)	0.005	(0.22)						
YRSEDUC	-0.005	(0.89)	-0.009	(3.18)	-0.011	(1.96)	-0.003	(0.81)	-0.008	(2.29)	-0.005	(1.02)
MOBRATE	-0.009	(2.21)	0.002	(0.46)	-0.012	(2.54)	-0.005	(1.66)	-0.004	(0.66)	-0.01	(2.11)
OWND	0.168	(2.15)	0.105	(1.63)	0.16	(2.05)	0.15	(2.19)	-0.08	(0.79)	0.19	(3.19)
LEGTEN	0.103	(1.23)	-0.08	(1.09)	-0.08	(0.60)	-0.09	(1.12)	0.16	(1.66)	-0.019	(0.24)
HOUSESZ	0.002	(1.43)	-0.0002	(0.30)	0.0005	(1.39)	0.0006	(0.65)	0.0005	(0.49)	0.0002	(0.55)
PRPROOM	-0.009	(0.39)	-0.46	(2.64)	-0.049	(3.11)	-0.02	(1.53)	-0.07	(2.67)	-0.04	(2.21)
DWAGE	0.0003	(1.03)	0.00003	(0.12)	0.0004	(2.25)	0.0005	(1.84)	0.0004	(1.16)	0.0003	(1.44)

Table A6.4b contd.

Variable Name	Income			Stage in Life Cycle		
	0 to 700	701 to 1500	1501 or more	Young	Mature	Old
STRUQ	0.034 (1.36)	0.09 (4.11)	0.11 (2.95)	0.09 (4.22)	0.84 (1.12)	0.069 (2.66)
SURFQ	0.015 (0.81)	-0.02 (1.06)	-0.047 (1.30)	0.02 (1.01)	-0.02 (0.77)	-0.01 (0.54)
UTILQ	0.008 (0.52)	0.009 (0.64)	-0.015 (0.94)	-0.0009 (0.07)	0.009 (0.51)	0.014 (0.93)
TRTMHD	0.004 (1.76)	-0.001 (0.85)	-0.0009 (0.62)	0.002 (1.39)	-0.002 (0.83)	-0.0006 (0.45)
WALLD	-0.605 (3.33)	0.250 (2.04)	-0.264 (3.09)	-0.29 (2.77)	-0.07 (0.54)	-0.04 (0.45)
UPINCD	0.096 (1.13)	0.08 (1.17)	0.002 (0.03)	0.04 (0.58)	0.11 (1.24)	0.05 (0.80)
INTERCEPT	-0.031	-0.024	0.417	-0.404	0.515	0.038
R-SQUARE	0.31	0.24	0.29	0.29	0.21	0.27
F-RATIO	4.25	4.43	5.84	5.69	2.83	5.36
N	177	239	248	229	184	251

Note: Figures in parenthesis are 't' values.

TABLE A6.5a
Determinants of Potential Mobility Status—SET C
DEPENDENT VARIABLE: MOBILITY STATUS
CONSTRAINED IMMOBILE = 0, STATISFIED IMMOBILE = 1

Variable Name	Total Samples		House Type		Tenure	
			Huts, Chawls, Pols	Others	Renter	Owner
INCOME	−0.000014	(1.10)	−0.00001 (0.39)	−0.00002 (1.24)	−0.0001 (2.81)	−0.000002 (0.20)
HSEXP2	0.000082	(2.02)	0.0005 (3.09)	0.00004 (1.13)	0.0006 (3.39)	0.00005 (1.24)
HHSIZE	0.00659	(1.18)	−0.0005 (0.42)	0.02 (3.10)	0.02 (1.14)	0.0006 (1.03)
STLIFE	0.0169	(1.51)	0.03 (2.00)	0.007 (0.52)	0.02 (0.89)	0.02 (1.45)
YRSEDUC	−0.00047	(0.20)	−0.002 (0.58)	0.002 (0.69)	−0.0006 (0.22)	−0.003 (0.71)
MOBRATE	−0.00303	(2.46)	−0.002 (1.12)	−0.003 (1.00)	−0.002 (1.08)	−0.005 (2.03)
OWND	0.2177	(6.09)	0.25 (5.00)	0.17 (2.96)	—	—
LEGTEN	−0.0494	(1.08)	−0.12 (1.96)	−0.17 (1.47)	−0.06 (0.96)	−0.008 (0.12)
HOUSESZ	0.00014	(0.60)	−0.00001 (0.03)	0.0002 (0.59)	−0.00003 (0.83)	0.0003 (1.18)
PRPROOM	−0.0281	(3.03)	0.0005 (0.04)	−0.08 (4.27)	−0.03 (1.52)	−0.03 (2.47)
DWAGE	0.00019	(1.64)	0.0002 (1.55)	−0.0006 (2.55)	0.00009 (0.45)	0.0002 (1.69)

Table A6.5a contd.

Variable Name	Total Samples		House Type		Tenure	
			Huts, Chawls, Pols	Others	Renter	Owner
STRUQ	0.0663	(4.93)	0.002 (0.11)	0.06 (1.99)	0.04 (1.59)	0.07 (4.02)
SURFQ	0.00175	(0.15)	0.04 (2.19)	−0.01 (0.67)	0.04 (2.12)	−0.02 (1.09)
UTILQ	0.0115	(1.42)	0.03 (2.47)	−0.02 (1.48)	0.021 (1.61)	0.01 (1.26)
TRTMHD	0.001	(1.18)	0.001 (0.88)	0.0005 (0.55)	0.0001 (0.68)	0.001 (1.04)
WALLD	−0.2039	(3.81)	—	—	−0.155 (1.74)	0.23 (3.40)
UPINCD	0.0746	(1.38)	—	—	0.133 (1.65)	0.08 (1.82)
INTERCEPT	−0.2521		−0.344	0.384	−0.47	0.055
R-SQUARE	0.29		0.21	0.22	0.209	0.23
F-RATIO	16.5		5.69	6.89	3.91	8.55
N	710		341	369	253	457

Note: Figures in parenthesis are 't' values.

TABLE A6.5b

Variable Name	Income			Stage in Life Cycle		
	0 to 700	701 to 1500	1501 or more	Young	Mature	Old
INCOME	0.00007 (1.03)	-0.000003 (0.02)	0.0001 (2.42)	-0.00003 (1.30)	-0.00002 (0.58)	-0.000005 (0.29)
HSEXP2	0.015 (1.69)	0.01 (0.65)	-0.012 (1.30)	0.00009 (1.49)	0.0001 (1.30)	0.00002 (0.28)
HHSIZE	0.037 (1.68)	0.012 (0.52)	0.02 (0.92)	0.009 (1.22)	-0.02 (1.85)	0.005 (0.40)
STLIFE						
YRSEDUC	-0.0003 (0.09)	0.0010 (0.18)	-0.004 (0.78)	-0.002 (0.61)	-0.008 (1.08)	0.003 (0.65)
MOBRATE	-0.003 (1.69)	-0.005 (1.57)	-0.006 (1.42)	-0.003 (2.20)	-0.009 (1.75)	-0.004 (0.61)
OWND	0.204 (3.03)	0.15 (2.51)	0.34 (5.20)	0.19 (3.32)	0.22 (3.28)	0.28 (4.69)
LEGTEN	0.05 (0.62)	-0.146 (1.84)	-0.19 (1.64)	-0.03 (0.45)	-0.05 (0.64)	0.0002 (0.02)
HOUSESZ	-0.0001 (0.29)	-0.0004 (0.48)	0.0004 (1.33)	0.001 (1.68)	-0.0003 (1.01)	0.0005 (1.52)
PRPROOM	-0.037 (1.84)	-0.0404 (2.35)	-0.01 (0.76)	-0.02 (1.17)	-0.47 (2.63)	0.001 (0.07)
DWAGE	0.0001 (0.46)	0.0003 (1.11)	0.0001 (0.78)	0.0003 (1.48)	-0.0003 (1.51)	0.0003 (2.08)
STRUQ	0.053 (2.37)	0.07 (3.01)	0.08 (2.70)	0.09 (4.05)	0.039 (1.59)	0.06 (2.48)
SURFQ	0.009 (0.51)	0.006 (0.31)	0.005 (0.15)	-0.004 (0.20)	0.009 (0.42)	-0.01 (0.50)
UTILQ	0.005 (0.38)	0.032 (2.22)	-0.025 (1.48)	-0.01 (0.91)	0.02 (1.57)	0.047 (3.21)
TRTMHD	-0.0003 (0.20)	0.002 (1.31)	0.0003 (0.22)	0.002 (1.34)	0.001 (0.66)	-0.0003 (0.18)
WALLD	-0.38 (3.10)	-0.12 (1.29)	-0.23 (2.74)	-0.17 (1.29)	-0.20 (1.96)	-0.30 (3.52)
UPINCD	0.010 (0.13)	0.16 (2.22)	-0.009 (0.15)	0.096 (1.41)	0.011 (0.14)	0.039 (0.59)
INTERCEPT	-0.2003	-0.413	-0.053	-0.30	0.29	-0.39
R-SQUARE	0.34	0.22	0.37	0.31	0.38	0.29
F-RATIO	6.09	4.53	9.41	6.51	7.07	6.28
N	203	267	240	254	201	255

Note: Figures in parenthesis are 't' values.

7. Housing Adjustment Processes

Housing is not just a commodity but a dynamic activity, and therefore, households undertake a variety of measures to adjust their housing consumption over time. The major focus of most studies dealing with housing adjustment mechanisms has been on residential mobility (c.f. Rossi (1955), Abu-Lughod and Foley (1960), Brown and Moore (1970), Quigley and Weinberg (1977), etc.). Such studies assume that 'the extent to which the family can alter its consumption of housing services without moving is quite limited' (Goodman, 1976). However, as indicated earlier, the incidence of mobility is quite limited amongst the Ahmedabad households, a fact which suggests that there are also other mechanisms adopted by the household to alter its housing consumption. An understanding of the household's adjustment process can help in identifying the household behaviour in a constrained market and provide certain policy directions to facilitate such a process.

Nature of Housing Adjustments

In the previous chapter focus was on the decision making contexts which lead the households to contemplate change. Extending this framework further, it is possible to discuss the second stage of housing adjustment as a choice between alternatives of moving, improving or a combination of both. This choice depends on both the household's own perceptions about the costs and benefits associated with each alternative and the prevalent market conditions (Seek, 1983). However, this decision is also critically linked to the main motivation for seeking a housing adjustment.

The two basic processes of housing adjustments are residential mobility and upgradation. It is also likely that some households may combine both strategies over their housing careers. Other remaining households are likely to be either completely satisfied with their housing situation or those who have adjusted their aspirations due to the severity of constraints.

A little over one-third of the households in Ahmedabad have made no active housing adjustments involving neither move nor upgradation. About one-fourth have moved and a slightly higher proportion have upgraded their houses and only about 10 per cent have both moved and upgraded the house. We have examined the characteristics of these different groups to understand their process of housing adjustment.

The salient characteristics of these various adjustors are presented in Table 7.1. It is seen that mobility as a mode of housing adjustment is typically adopted by non-poor migrant households who were initially in the formal rental market. The major motivation for this group appears to be to own a shelter. This is evident from the proportion of owner households which increases from

TABLE 7.1

Salient Household Characteristics by Adjustment Processes

Characteristics	Adjustment Processes				
	Move (N=234)	Upgrade (N=265)	Move and Upgrade (N=94)	Passive (N=340)	Total (N=933)
1. Percentage migrant households	70.09	40.00	55.32	51.47	53.27
2. Percentage of households below Rs. 700 household monthly income	21.37	36.98	30.85	25.88	28.40
3 Percentage of households in informal housing	31.20	56.23	76.60	27.30	41.47
4 Percentage of owner households at entry into housing market	18.80	64.13	6.38	62.94	n.a.
5 Percentage of owner households at present	58.0	64.13	53.0	62.94	61.00
6 Current mean monthly per capita income in Rupees	330	222	231	356	299

19 per cent at the time of entry to 58 per cent. An even more dramatic increase in ownership is evident among the mover-cum-upgrader group.

Upgradation strategy, on the other hand, seems to be largely adopted by the poor, non-migrant households who are owners of informal housing. A crucial aspect in the upgradation process appears to be security of tenure. The mover-upgrader category is characteristic of the housing adjustment strategy adopted by the urban poor. They appear to move to a 'secure' site either through squatting or purchasing the land from quasi-legal developers. The shelter upgradation, which is a gradual process, then takes place according to space availability and the household's ability to mobilise finances.

The passive adjusters are largely the non-poor, owner households who may be classified as the satisfied immobile group. These households, by virtue of their ownership of formal sector housing, either do not have any scope for upgradation in the shelter or are satisfied by altering their aspiration regions with the dynamic changes in the household characteristics instead of altering their housing situation. Thus, the housing adjustment modes vary across households by their tenure status, income levels and the nature of shelter. These aggregate characteristics, however, do not provide adequate understanding of each process. In the analysis below, the process of mobility and upgradation is examined in more detail. For the purpose of this analysis, the mover-upgrader households have been clubbed with movers or upgraders as relevant.

Residential Mobility in Ahmedabad

The empirical evidence suggests that mobility as a mode of housing adjustment has been used only by one-third of the city households. Further, a bulk of the mover households have moved only once during their entire housing career. Mobility thus appears to be a less preferred or feasible strategy of housing adjustment. During the last five years, only about 8.4 per cent of the households have moved giving an average of only about 1.7 per cent per annum. These low mobility rates are suggestive of the serious constraints faced by households in finding adequate housing at the desired location within affordable prices. Alternatively, as discussed in the previous chapter, those who are protected under Rent Control

Act are likely to either not move despite the need and potential or at least defer the decision for as long as possible.

Amongst the mobile households, it is interesting to know the variation in the mobility rate by the period of entry into the housing market. Table 7.2, presents the mobility rates of different cohorts which relate to the duration of stay of the household in the city. In the case of the migrant household, the duration of stay is

TABLE 7.2
Extent of Mobility Among Households by Household Age

Household age in the city (years)	No. of moves since formation of household					Total
	No move	One	Two	Three	More than three	
0 to 5	91.74	4.26	0.8	1.6	1.6	100.0 (121)
6 to 10	72.11	17.68	6.80	1.36	2.05	100.0 (147)
11 to 15	61.88	24.38	9.37	1.87	2.50	100.0 (160)
16 to 20	63.23	25.80	5.81	2.58	2.58	100.0 (155)
21 to 25	52.73	28.78	8.22	8.22	2.05	100.0 (146)
26 or more	55.88	25.00	7.35	5.39	6.38	100.0 (204)
Total	64.84	21.75	6.64	3.64	3.11	100.0 (933)

Note: In this and subsequent tables, the household age is as of 1984, the year of survey.

clearly defined. For non-migrant households, the household head's entry into the labour market is taken as the surrogate for determining the household's stay in the city. This duration of stay in the housing market is termed as household age. The propensity to move is seen to increase with household age as evident from the declining proportion of the non-movers with increase in household age.

Even though mobility rates are low in recent years, it is likely that the housing market situation would have some effect on this.

For example, Edwards (1983) found that, 'among Bucaramangua's low income population, the age at which home ownership has usually been attained has varied significantly over the last fifty years'. He asserts that 'when prices are low in real terms, "poorer" and "younger" families are able to own property'. This analysis shows that while the mean household age at the first move increases with an increase in the household age; it appears that for a majority of the mover households, the first move was made during the decade of 1970–80. During this period, the city of Ahmedabad also witnessed a significant accrual to the housing stock as a result of the housing cooperative movement and in the latter part of the decade through the exemptions of the Urban Land Ceiling and Regulations Act of 1976. This suggests that, though the socio-demographic factors play an important role in determining the preference structure of the households, the market conditions facilitate (or influence) the actual decision to move.

ADJUSTMENTS THROUGH MOBILITY BY VARIOUS COHORTS

While the general picture at the aggregate level suggests that most mobile households have improved their housing situation after the move, it is of some interest to examine these characteristics at the disaggregated level for different cohorts (Table 7.3). It is found that a much smaller proportion of recent households have managed to become owners as compared to the older households. A majority of these older households have shifted their location from the walled city to other parts of the city. The recent households, however, appear to be moving within the zone of previous residence and a majority of them appear to be concentrated in eastern Ahmedabad and the eastern peripheral areas. Eastern sector of the city thus appears to be both a reception zone for the new migrant households as well as those who aspire to become owners. Older households have also managed to improve the quality of shelter, both in terms of the type of shelter and the built-up area of the shelter, while the more recent households have managed only marginal improvements.

The experience of various cohorts suggests that the housing adjustment behaviour is increasingly being governed by the market related factors. The more recent households are constrained to adjust their housing situation within the same segment of the market. Ownership of shelter also appears to be more difficult for

TABLE 7.3
Housing Adjustment Process of Movers by Different Cohorts

Characteristics	Year in the housing market (household age)					Total (all movers)
	Less than 10 years (N=51)	*10 to 15 years* (N=61)	*16 to 20 years* (N=57)	*21 to 25 years* (N=69)	*More than 25 years* (N=90)	(N=328)
1. Percentage of migrant households	74.51	73.77	56.14	65.21	62.21	65.85
2. *Tenure*						
a. Percentage of owner households at entry	1.96	8.20	7.20	10.14	13.33	8.87
b. Percentage of owner households at present	41.18	50.82	63.16	73.91	62.22	59.45
3. *Location** Percentage of households residing in:						
a. *at entry:*						
Walled city	5.88	8.2	17.54	34.78	28.89	20.73
East AMC	52.94	40.98	45.61	34.78	46.95	46.95
West AMC	11.76	11.48	15.79	11.54	10.67	10.67
East Periphery	17.65	29.51	12.88	10.14	14.33	14.33
West Periphery	7.84	3.28	—	1.45	2.13	2.13
b. Walled city	1.96	3.28	1.75	7.25	4.44	3.69
East AMC	56.86	34.43	38.60	39.13	53.33	44.82
West AMC	11.76	19.67	28.07	23.19	15.56	19.51
East Periphery	21.57	37.70	28.07	13.04	20.10	23.48
West Periphery	7.84	4.92	3.51	17.39	36.67	8.23
4. *House Type** Percentage of household staying in:						
a. *at entry:*						
Informal	35.30	49.18	43.86	43.47	46.67	44.21
Pol	11.76	11.48	14.04	31.88	23.33	19.51
Formal	52.94	39.34	42.10	24.65	30.00	41.28
b. *at present:*						
Informal*	35.29	47.54	43.86	34.78	31.11	37.87
Pol	11.76	6.56	1.75	5.80	3.33	5.49
Formal	52.94	45.90	54.39	59.42	65.56	56.70
5. *Shelter size in sq. mts:*						
a. at entry	25.45	24.36	33.23	29.16	26.61	28.81
b. at present	28.38	29.60	51.49	52.81	46.21	42.65

Note: Figures in items 1 to 4 are percentages to mover households in each cohort.
* Percentage may not add up to 100.0 due to those not responding.

TABLE 7.4
Nature of Upgradation by House Type

Nature of Upgradation	Percentage of upgrading households to total households residing in:			Total
	Informal* housing	Pol housing	Formal* housing	
1. Increase in size of shelter	9.38	14.28	59.62	24.50
2. Changes in the wall/ roof materials	35.96	10.78	0.0	22.60
3. Changes in flooring/ wall finishing and alterations	24.88	28.89	30.46	26.96
4. Improvement in services—water, sanitation/ drainage at household level	84.03	30.95	15.00	57.78
Sample of upgrading households	213	42	104	359

* Informal here refers to huts and chawls whereas formal refers to the other house types.

these recent households as compared to the older households. Though a majority of these recent households are migrants to the city, their initial locations are restricted to eastern Ahmedabad, where the rents and house prices are relatively lower.

The older households, on the other hand, have probably benefited by the relatively low house price-income ratios that prevailed in the early seventies along with the liberal finance available from housing cooperative finance agencies. With these the older households were in a position to choose the location type of shelter and the size of the house.

Upgradation Process

The scant literature available on upgradation or home improvement is reflective of the fact that most governments in developing countries have overlooked the need for upgradation of existing housing stock. Upgradation has only recently been accepted by these governments, often because of the availability of international assistance. Researchers have defined upgradation in different ways. Struyk (1982), for example, only views addition to dwelling area as a process of upgradation in Korean cities. Seek (1983) also looks at additional areas or alteration in dwelling as an home improvement process in Adelaide, Australia. The bulk of the literature related to squatter upgradation (e.g., Turner 1976) has concentrated on the shelter improvement alone. Studies by Jimminez (1982) and Strassman (1982) have taken a more comprehensive view of upgradation in their evaluation of the squatter upgradation. In consonance with these recent studies, we have characterised the upgradation process as either an increase in the size of the shelter, improvement in shelter quality or an improvement in housing services. In the analysis presented below, the upgrader and mover-upgrader households have been pooled together.

NATURE OF UPGRADATION

At the aggregate level, improvement in levels of services is the most prevalent mode of upgradation. However, when the upgradation processes by the segments of the housing market is examined, a different picture emerges. The predominant mode of upgradation in the informal settlements appears to be with regard to improvements in the level of services. This is largely on account of the environmental improvement schemes undertaken by the Municipal Corporation during the seventies in which public amenities as well as shelter level amenities were provided.

In these informal settlements only a small proportion of households have managed to increase the dwelling area. This reflects the severe space constraint in informal settlements. On the other hand, nearly 60 per cent of the upgraders in the formal sector have been able to increase the shelter size. The other form of upgradation in the formal sector appears to be that of improvement in the exterior quality of shelter, such as the flooring/wall finishing.

Upgradation as a strategy of housing adjustment thus appears to be prevalent in all sections of the market. The nature of upgradation, however, differs across various sections depending upon the constraints of space, availability of finance and preferences. It may be recalled that nearly 40 per cent of the upgraders are not the owners of their shelter. Their tenure status may also have been a constraint in upgradation behaviour.

The extent of upgradation carried out by these households is also influenced by these factors. In the informal sector, there is a significant increase in the proportion of households that have added services, like water taps, drainage and electricity. Changes in the quality of roof seem more pronounced than the changes in the wall material. Many informal houses have also improved the exterior quality of shelter using whitewash/or paint.

Pol housing, which are traditional residential areas, were designed more than a century ago and the process of provision of basic services such as toilets, water taps and the like, has been a gradual one. The extent of upgradation on shelter quality or size is marginal. Majority of the upgrader households in the formal sector have increased the size of shelter. On an average, these households have added a room of 12.5 sq.mts. to the initial shelter. These households have also improved the shelter quality over the years by changing the roofing material and improving the external finishes.

FINANCING OF UPGRADATION

One of the major difficulties associated with examining the upgradation processes, particularly in the informal sector housing, relates to the estimation of the cost of improvements. This is primarily due to the fact that upgradation is a gradual process and in a cross-sectional study conducted at a later date, recall problems make it difficult to ascertain the costs associated with upgradation. Secondly, the building materials used in upgradation are often acquired through non-market transactions like gifts or thefts.

The informal housing dwellers in Ahmedabad have spent, on an average Rs. 500 to Rs. 1000, over a period of two to five years for the 'initial' improvements in the walls and roof. Usually such improvement is financed through their own savings. The next stage of upgradation, related to changes in flooring, addition to the built-up area, exterior finishes etc., is a one-shot operation involving an outlay of Rs. 3000 to Rs. 5000. For those households which have an earning member employed in the formal sector, such expenditure is usually financed through loans from employer. For the other households, such improvements occur only after

TABLE 7.5
Details of Upgradation Undertaken

Attributes of Upgradation	Informal		Pol		Formal	
	Current	Initial	Current	Initial	Current	Initial
1. Increase in size (built-up area in sq. mts.) (For those who have made improvement)	32.0	24.8	38.0	30.2	48.0	35.5
2. Changes in wall material						
a Percentage of houses with mud/cloth/wood planks	6.57	29.72	—	—	—	—
b Brick walls	41.78	28.17	100.00	80.77	—	—
3. Changes in roofing Percentage of houses with AC sheets/tiles	85.45	65.72	55.29	66.67	2.88	22.12
4 Changes in flooring						
a Percentage of houses with mud flooring	20.66	63.85	1.90	14.29	—	—
b Polished tiles	19.25	13.62	54.77	40.48	79.81	68.27
5 Changes in wall finish						
a Percentage of households with no plaster on walls	21.60	47.42	—	—	—	—
b Whitewash/paint	63.38	25.82	97.62	90.48	94.96	74.04
6. Services related						
a Percentage of houses with individual water taps	66.67	4.69	80.95	54.76	—	—
b Drainage connection	72.93	9.38	88.10	76.19	90.38	66.35
c Individual toilets	27.70	11.74	71.43	64.29	96.16	71.27
d Electricity	63.38	14.55	100.0	70.50	100.0	100.00

about 10 to 15 years in the city and at a stage when the household incomes are steady as well as comparable to the formal sector employment. Such households typically pool their family savings and supplement the small funds by borrowings from friends and relatives. None of the sample households appear to have borrowed from money lenders for home upgradation. Our results closely match with the earlier detailed studies of upgradation in Ahmedabad (cf. Sharma, 1983 and Mehta and Mehta, 1987). In the formal housing sector, since an increase in shelter size or improvement in shelter quality required an expenditure of Rs. 10,000 to Rs. 20,000, nearly half the upgraders financed this expenditure through loans from employer whilst the rest used their own savings for this purpose.

On the whole, it is seen that only the formal sector employees have been able to mobilise the requisite finances for upgradation from their employers. Households, particularly in the informal sector, by and large depend on their meagre savings or seek the help of friends and relatives. The nature of upgradation in the informal housing sector is thus extremely constrained due to lack of adequate finance. A housing finance system which provides short-term loans with flexible repayment schedules would significantly enhance the nature and extent of upgradation in this sector.

TENURE SECURITY AND UPGRADATION

There is an unanimous consensus regarding the positive association between tenure security and upgradation (e.g., Turner, 1972 and Jimminez, 1982). The perception of tenure security is necessary before any substantial home improvements are made. This perceived security of tenure, in the context of Ahmedabad, is inadvertently granted by the Municipal Corporation as it undertook a slum census survey in 1976 and issued identity cards. Also, a majority of the slum settlements have been provided public toilets and water taps by the Corporation. Provision of these facilities have considerably reduced the threats of eviction and as a consequence, a large proportion of slum dwellers have begun improvements in their shelter.

A majority of the slum improvement programmes in India require transfer of ownership rights of land to the slum dwellers which is then used as a collateral for home improvement loans. Such a transfer adversely affects the renter households in these slums who are either forcefully evicted or required to pay higher rents (cf. Kalyani, 1986). The extent of upgradation between slums which have legal rights over land and those which do not is not significantly different (see Risbud, 1987, for a study of Bhopal in Madhya Pradesh). It appears that the perception of security in terms of extremely low risks of eviction are necessary and sufficient for slum households to be motivated for home upgradation.

Summary

The analysis in this chapter has focused on the two main processes of housing adjustments, namely, mobility and upgradation. On the whole, in Ahmedabad, a little over one-third of the households have made no housing adjustment at all. Of the rest, some 15 per cent have moved as well as upgraded, whereas others are almost equally divided amongst the processes of mobility and upgradation.

Residential mobility is apparently a more successful type of housing adjustment and is directed at becoming owners. The effect of market forces is evident as a large proportion of these movers had moved during the seventies when there was a considerable increase in the supply and the house price-income ratio was lower. Spatially, the movement has been either out of the walled city or confined to the same sectors. Mobility has meant housing improvements for most households, although about 20 per cent have moved to inferior house types or smaller dwellings. Another important finding relates to the predominance of migrants amongst movers. Although for the entire city only about 53 per cent of the head of households are migrants, this proportion rises to two-thirds amongst movers and to about three-fourths for the recent movers.

Compared to mobility, the rates for housing upgradation are even lower with almost 60 per cent of households not having made any progress in this direction. Although minor repairs and maintenance may certainly be an on-going process, very few households seem to be making major changes in their housing. Upgradation as a strategy is prevalent in different sub-markets but the nature of upgradation is quite distinct. Amongst the 'informal' settlements, the level of services has improved although this is largely due to external inputs by public agencies. A significant proportion of informal settlement households have improved the material quality of shelter. On the other hand, in the formal housing sector a number of households have added a room to their house. The financing for these processes has largely come from either own savings, relatives, or from the employers. Institutional finance for housing can be made available for upgradation to encourage and motivate a large number of households who are at present constrained to undertake home improvements.

The residential processes are greatly affected by the overall situation, both of housing and the urban economy in general. In Ahmedabad, a large proportion of the households do not undergo substantial housing adjustments. The restrictive housing behaviour is, of course, much more pronounced as one goes down the income strata and goes up the household age or year of entry in the housing market. First, only the relatively upper-income strata are able to achieve improvements or good housing situation. Households in the middle-income strata are able to achieve satisfactory conditions only when they are 'lucky' enough to get institutional support. It is very important to understand the demonstration effect of such 'success stories' on their housing aspirations. Thus, these households tend to have high expectations regardless of the actual achievements. On the other hand, the preference structure changes considerably amongst the lower income strata. First of all, they would generally like to minimise their housing expenditure and, second, they are more ready to (or rather forced to) adjust their housing aspirations. They are further constrained by their need to maintain high accessibility to employment.

On the whole, the residential behaviour in relation to the preferences and constraints suggest certain distinct patterns of household behaviour as emerging within the context of local housing market in Ahmedabad. There are four such stylised typologies as described below:

Early achievers belong either to the upper-income group households who with their greater resources manage to achieve satisfactory housing at an early age or those few who are lucky enough to gain access to limited, subsidised public housing or inherit good housing.

Middle-age or late achievers are those who manage to achieve good and satisfactory housing but only after initial struggles. These may comprise of either those who manage to continue in good jobs or are able to save enough at least at later stages as well as gain access to housing finance. Quite often, they may simply scrape through by the combined income of an extended family. The actual improvement may come largely through residential mobility. A few who are in a favourable location and tenure situation may also attempt upgradation.

Constrained adjusters are those who due to various reasons are simply unable to attain good and satisfactory housing. Their constraints force them to adjust their housing aspirations considerably or to make trade-offs on the different preferences and the level of housing expenditures. These may comprise of two types of households: those who face severe constraints of actual and/or perceived opportunities due to either stagnant or falling real incomes and the continued priority for work accessibility. These groups are then forced to continue in the same house, adjust their aspirations and make do with small housing adjustments. The second group, however, may be those affected by institutional factors like rent control legislation and/or lack of access to housing finance. Thus, these households may be adjusting their aspirations due to the large gap between current housing expenditure and prevailing prices in relation to likely utility improvements. Similarly, lack of access to housing finance limits the effective affordability, especially within the ownership market and thus forces these households to become constrained adjusters.

Downward mobile are those whose housing situation may actually worsen over time. They also may comprise of two types, those who are literally forced out of their house (to a worse one) due to economic factors of 'unaffordable opportunity costs' or due to contextual factors like riots and evictions. In Ahmedabad, although the state operated evictions have been extremely limited, riots, which are becoming increasingly common, have often had their basis in property relations (see, Engineer, 1985). The downward mobility, however, may also occur in the same house in different ways. With falling real incomes the household may be unable to keep up the necessary improvements in relation to the life cycle of both the family and the house. On the other hand, the particular physical (or spatial) or legal context of the house may not permit improvements, especially in size, individual services and quality despite improvements in income. In both these cases, the actual housing situation will tend to worsen.

The distribution of households in these different stylised groups will be critically linked both to the buoyancy of the local economy and to the public policy. It is obvious that in a buoyant economy, larger and larger proportions would be able to move to higher processes. On the contrary, in a declining economy, greater numbers will be forced in the latter (lower) processes.

8. Findings and Policy Directions

A review of urban housing policies in post-independence India reveals that there is a very definite move towards a support policy framework, while at the same time it is realised that a completely top-down perspective with policies emanating from the Centre is untenable, especially as the local housing context is extremely important. However, both these aspects necessitate an understanding of local housing markets. We have attempted to gain insights into this important area of research through this exploratory study of Ahmedabad Housing Market, the major findings of which are presented here.

DISPARATE RESIDENTIAL STRUCTURE OF AHMEDABAD

Ahmedabad, like most metropolises in developing countries, has a distinctly segregated residential structure. Most of this development has occurred in this century following the high population growth due to the development of the textile industry at the turn of the century. Since independence, while the city has experienced a moderate growth rate of population, each of the sub-zones of the city shows variations in the growth and the nature of development. The fort walls, which essentially houses middle-income households, has had a net decline of population, whereas the eastern peripheral areas, which accommodate a majority of the city's poorer households, have witnessed a proliferation of slums and other low income housing in the last two decades. The western areas housing the elite in the past, are now growing rapidly due to the middle and upper-income group housing activity.

Although in terms of aggregate statistics, almost 40 per cent of the total stock consists of huts and chawls which represent inferior house types, the quality of stock in terms of building materials is not very poor. Only 8 per cent of the houses have undurable (*kutcha*) walls and roof while about 20 per cent of the houses have brick walls with *kutcha* roof. The structural conditions, however, in huts, chawls and pols are quite poor, which together comprise about 50 per cent of the total stock. In terms of the infrastructure situation, access to water supply, seems quite adequate. Almost 75 per cent of the households have individual water taps and another 20 per cent at least have an access to the public taps. Even in hutments, almost 88 per cent of the households have some access to water supply. However, nearly half of the city's population does not have a private toilet and more seriously 15 per cent do not even have access to a public toilet. It should be remembered that most of the public toilets are poorly maintained and the effective access is limited. Even access to public water taps, constitutes an inconvenient and constrained situation due to limited hours of supply.

Compared to the above attributes, the average situation in terms of the tenure and house size appear to be very good on the face of it. In 1981, according to the property tax records of Ahmedabad Municipal Corporation (which excludes a large proportion of the slum areas), about 36 per cent of the houses were self-owned, which compares very favourably with the other metropolises in India. Our survey results, including the informal sector and the agglomerated peripheral areas, suggest that almost 60 per cent of the households were owner-occupiers.

These encouraging averages, however, hide the underlying distributional problems. Of these, the ownership by the lower income strata is generally achieved only in the informal sector. Although in the local political climate, these groups have enjoyed a high level of security of tenure, in the next decade its future is bleak in the light of a faltering urban economy and extensive commercialisation of the housing processes. There are ominous signs coming from other states regarding the forceful eviction of the so-called slum dwellers especially in Maharashtra and Karnataka.

The disparities in the distribution of housing resources is also very clearly evident with respect to housing size. Although the average house size in Ahmedabad stands at a very reasonable 50 sq.m., almost two-thirds of the households live in houses below this size. More than 40 per cent live in houses with less than 25 sq.m. of area. Similarly, even in terms of per capita availability of built-up space, 50 per cent of the households have less than 5.5 sq.m. of space.

The reasons for these spatial and economic disparities in access to housing services relates to the nature of housing supplies in

Ahmedabad. The access to formal recognised sector, with a better level of housing services, has been largely limited to the upper-middle and upper-income groups. Besides the economic capacity necessary to enter this sector, even the information about these opportunities is not easily available. Even the public sector opportunities accrue only to a few lucky ones, as its contribution has been very limited. Most of the lower-income groups are thus dependent on the informal sector with its low level of housing services. In recent years, even the popular control and flexibility, once the major advantages, are fast becoming a total myth. Quasi-legal developers have essentially taken over the housing supply of this sector.

URBAN ECONOMY AND HOUSING DEVELOPMENTS

The nature of housing developments, even in a local housing market, are greatly influenced by the changing structure of the urban economy, macro-economic forces and the nature of the public policy. Ahmedabad has been largely a textile city, with almost one-fourth of the city's income being generated directly by this sector. Other manufacturing and service sectors are strongly interdependent on textiles. It was the growth and boom in textiles in the pre-independence period, which led to the phenomenal growth of population in the thirties. Since then, however, Ahmedabad has maintained an almost steady but moderate rate of growth. However, there is an indication of a slight downward trend in the last decade.

The city's textile industry was probably at its peak somewhere in the first half of seventies. However, since then there has been a stagnation in this sector leading to a closure of twenty-two mills in the eighties. During the seventies, there has been more growth in employment in the informal sector (cf. Mehta, 1982a). The influence of these trends on the city's overall economy is likely to be quite serious. The city's income has probably declined significantly in this period. The effects of these trends on the housing activity have been substantial.

The fifties and sixties witnessed a high growth in housing by upper-income groups supported by the institutional housing finance from the Apex Cooperative Housing Society. Most of this was concentrated in the relatively 'better' areas in western Ahmedabad. During this period, housing was mostly developed by the user groups themselves. Gradually, however, with the increasing urban activity, the profits from land and property price increases were well above returns from other similar investments. At this stage, with the textile sector still doing well, the surplus generation in this sector (especially the unofficial or 'black' component) became available for the attractive real estate sector. On the other hand, with technological developments, increasing prices and greater complexities in the construction or residential development process necessitated the entry of professionals as a major actor group. The seventies thus saw a major shift in the nature of residential development processes which were largely user-controlled to an increasing commercialisation by builders and developers. This was further facilitated by legislations like Vacant Land Act of 1972 and, of course, the Urban Land (Ceiling and Regulations) Act in 1976. With these the speculative investments, which were so far confined largely to land, were now diverted to the booming housing market which promised high and relatively safe returns. This essentially led to the greater commercialisation and commodification of housing. The market values now dominated over the use value for the housing product.

This process has led to the entry of private firms into the housing market in a dominant way. At the same time, in the informal sector, slum-lordism and quasi-legal developments are now becoming more commonplace. This process of commoditisation is probably not restricted to the flow of new housing but also affects the existing stock, especially in areas where effective and representative community control is lacking. The highly celebrated popular sector of the sixties is fast becoming a myth in both the formal and informal sectors.

The slump in the textile sector, however, is now also affecting the nature of housing investments. The closure of many textile mills in the city has adversely affected the cycle of accumulation of surplus (especially in the parallel economy) and has created a serious cash-flow problem. On the whole, there is a general sense of despair about the city's economic well-being. This is further aggravated by the continuing disturbances and riots in the city. At the same time, in the economy at large, other more attractive investment possibilities (for the 'black' money) in the stock and bullion market are becoming available. This has probably affected the speculative housing demand in the city. Many housing projects have, thus, remained unsold or have been shelved, and the prices have not increased in the past three to four years. The market is again shifting back to needy buyers and is based on consumptive, rather than speculative demand.

DEMAND FOR HOUSING

In many of the local level housing strategies (and, at times, even in national estimates) there is a tendency to take a need-based approach without paying adequate attention to effective demand for housing services. Similarly, in most housing projects, there is a rather standardised assumption regarding housing demand. The question of housing preferences and the trade-offs amongst different services is generally left untouched. .

On the whole, the households in Ahmedabad spend very less towards their housing. The mean expenditure is Rs. 114 and median expenditure is Rs. 53. This, however, refers to the actual or out-of-pocket expenditure. If the opportunity cost of price paid for housing is imputed, the expenditure for owners increases almost threefold, though for the renters it remains the same. The median of housing expenditure as a proportion of household income is 4 per cent for renters and 12 per cent for the owners. There is a general decline in these proportions with an increase in income suggesting that the low-income groups spend a much larger proportion of their income (18 per cent) than the upper income groups (7 per cent). For owners, however, this ratio increases initially, with increases in income, and declines subsequently, suggesting that the marginal propensity to spend on ownership for the middle-income households appears to be high.

These results are better understood by an analysis of housing demand. The income elasticity of demand for owners is 0.2 and for renters, in the region of 0.17 to 0.40, depending upon the functional form of the demand equation. These results suggest a generally inelastic housing demand. However, when the income elasticity of demand for various income groups is examined, it emerges that for lower and middle-income renters, the income elasticity of demand is close to zero, and rises to 0.36 for higher income renters. On the other hand, for the owner households, the income elasticity is quite high (0.70) for the middle-income groups. Price, on the other hand, has a much greater influence on renter households. The price elasticity for renters is -0.8 and for owners only − 0.4. Besides these income and price effects, other aemographic variables like household size, stage in the life cycle, urban commitment and duration of residence also have a significant influence on housing demand. In addition, a very important factor is the potential access to housing finance which affects the demand significantly.

HOUSING PREFERENCES AND CONSTRAINTS

It is essential to understand the residential behaviour in a more disaggregated perspective by looking at the housing preferences and trade-offs amongst different housing attributes. The analysis of these aspects was based on the premise that there is a group of households who are in a state of disequilibrium. The differences between this group and the satisfied households are examined to derive housing preferences. Further, attention is also paid to the nature of constraints which affect these residential processes.

The highest priorities of most households seem to be for ownership and appropriate house size. However, the priority for ownership becomes more pronounced at later stages in the life cycle. This suggests a continuing need for rental housing for those in early stages in the life cycle which is generally ignored by most programmes. Although ownership is preferred by all, legal tenure is important only at later stages in the life cycle, if higher incomes are attained. Though size is a very important attribute of housing satisfaction, most households, except those in the highest income brackets, are unable to significantly improve on the initial conditions.

Shelter quality is important for middle and upper income strata while the lower income groups seem to trade-off shelter quality and tenure legality against work and social access. The need to be located near places of work goes beyond the obvious need to minimise the costs of travel. The nature of economic opportunities and, therefore, average earnings probably depend on appropriate location. Thus, in terms of stages of residential decision-making, the lower income groups seem to first decide on location and social access and trade-off other attributes against this. As against this, the middle-income strata start with searching for a house which maximises size within the bounds of their housing expenditure. At later stages in the life cycle, the other most important decision is ownership of house.

As against such preference patterns, the most important constraints relate to availability of and access to housing finance and information. Further, the residential processes are also greatly affected by the overall situation, both of housing and the urban economy in general. It is clear that the effects of restrictive situations are either to make the households constrained or to force them to adjust their aspirations. On the whole, it appears that the lower income groups tend to adjust their aspirations considerably so that their housing preferences appear to be distinct from the others. On the other hand, the middle-income groups have not adjusted their aspirations to a great extent. They are, therefore, much more likely to be either potentially mobile or feel constrained. Only the lucky ones who manage to gain access to either public housing or housing finance are able to acquire their aspired house, though generally only at later stages in the life cycle. Their expectations, however, continue to be above what they can actually achieve in the market. Only those with relatively high incomes are able to achieve satisfactory housing easily and at an early stage in their life cycle.

HOUSING ADJUSTMENTS

The highly constrained housing situation in Ahmedabad is evident from the low levels of housing adjustments through mobility or upgradation. About a third of the households have made no changes at all. However, a large proportion of this passive group is quite satisfied with their housing, suggesting early housing achievements. Residential mobility is also very restricted. Compared to the annual rate of around 10 to 12 per cent in western countries (Seek, 1983), only about 1.7 per cent of the households in Ahmedabad move each year. However, in a housing career perspective, residential mobility is apparently a more successful type of housing adjustment and is done mostly to achieve ownership. It is, of course, greatly affected by the market situation and a large proportion of the moves seem to have occurred in the seventies when there was a considerable increase in supply and easy access to institutional finance.

Housing upgradation as a strategy is prevalent in different submarkets but its nature is distinct. The material quality of shelter is improved by those in the informal settlements. On the other hand, increase in house size is more common in the formal housing and is rather restricted in the informal sector. Improvement in access to services in the latter is largely a reflection of the public policy rather than household efforts.

Emerging Policy Perspectives

The housing situation in a given urban area is critically linked to the overall conditions in the housing market and the buoyancy of the economy. Thus, minor tinkering with a few projects, no matter how innovative and successful they are, cannot comprise an adequate housing strategy. Even if minimum needs of only the lowest economic strata and the 'homeless' have to be met, it is essential to view the needs and especially housing demand of at least the middle income groups. Without such a perspective, no matter how well intended the programmes are, they will simply filter up in the light of the unfulfilled demand of the middle strata.

It is equally important to emphasise the role of the State within the framework of housing support policies. This emphasis visualises a drastic change in the State's role from that of a provider to a facilitator. We have seen earlier that the public sector has failed miserably in the former role in Ahmedabad. Its role as a facilitator necessitates housing support strategies which rely on indirect measures to influence the patterns of supply.

Metropolitan Ahmedabad is likely to double its population from 2.63 million in 1981 to 5.34 million in the year 2001, if it continues to grow at the present rate. Based on the past rates of household formation, there is likely to be a demand for nearly 3.45 lakh housing units in the decade of 1991–2001. This suggests gross land requirements of anywhere from 2500 to 6000 hectares, depending on the norms used.

As against the projected housing requirements for the decade, the average annual supply of formal sector housing in metropolitan Ahmedabad is likely to be 10,000 units based on past trends. Thus, at this rate, less than one-third of the housing requirement is likely to be met by formal sector housing in the next decade. The informal sector, which presumably would absorb the balance, also has a limited supply. Past records indicate that, on an average, about 5500 housing units are added by this sector each year.

It is thus likely that extensive sub-divisions of the existing stock will take place in response to the increasing pressures. A substantial proportion of the households will probably also have to double up in the existing stock and live in extremely crowded conditions. There are likely to be some imbalances in the different sub-markets. We have seen earlier that the formal sector has largely catered to higher and middle income strata only. Thus, unless the formal sector manages to change the nature of its product in response to the lower income group's preferences, there will probably be a glut in this sub-market. On the other hand, the quasi-legal development catering to the low-income groups will be much more successful. These processes already seem to be under-way in the Ahmedabad housing market as noticed in the inability of specific formal sector suppliers to sell houses (and/or plots) while quasi-legal developments are on the rise. The prices, on the other hand, are 'sticky' in the short run, though they may fall in real terms over a longer duration unless indirect tax measures render holding of vacant property expensive. Such imbalances may occur in specific sub-markets as delineated by the important attributes of location, tenure and shelter quality. The latter, of course, also influences the price and, therefore, the particular income group which has access to it. The access to housing finance is also a critical factor. The recent shortage of finance from the cooperative sector has also contributed to the glut in the market.

Given the scenario for the coming decade, the important questions that emerge are:

- What measures, direct and indirect, are necessary to ensure that adequate land will be available in the city for the requisite housing need?
- How will the demand for housing finance be met?
- How can the various supply systems in the city be influenced to facilitate a better matching of supplies with needs, preferences and demand while ensuring at least the basic minimum standards for the disadvantaged groups?
- What changes are necessary in specific legislations to reduce the inequities in the housing system while ensuring an overall growth?

A very detailed discussion of answers to these policy questions within the framework of an overall local housing strategy is certainly beyond the scope of this study. Our attempt here is to discuss the directions which emerge from our study.

While it is incorrect to state that the supply of urban land is inelastic, it is necessary to bear in mind that low-income families in Indian cities increasingly face serious problems in gaining access to land. Public policies must, therefore, recognise the need for providing land at reasonable rates to these households.

One of the direct measures to ensure such a land supply to the low-income households is through land readjustment or land pooling schemes. Many states in India, including Gujarat, have been practicing land readjustment in some form, within the available legislative framework. In Gujarat, recent amendments to the present Act empower the city authorities to reserve up to 10 per cent of land for low-income housing. Yet it is possible, within this Act, to undertake servicing of peripheral lands with full cost recovery from the original land owners and reserve lands for public purposes.

At the same time, indirect measures to facilitate utilisation of unbuilt floor space within the city would lead to more efficient use of the existing land resources. These indirect measures may be in terms of transfer of development rights, property taxation index at the level of utilisation of FSI or other similar measures.

More importantly, in the long term perspective, it is necessary to evolve a spatial structure which balances the location of major employment centres in the western zones and reduces the pressures on land in the eastern zones. It would be necessary to especially earmark adequate land for low-income housing near the proposed work areas. Thus both the urban land-use planning and the land readjustment scheme mechanisms should be effectively used to guide the pattern of development in a more balanced manner and ensuring access of low-income groups to land at the right time, place and prices.

Equally important, such serviced land must become available for development in the market. Our analysis of Urban Land Ceiling in Ahmedabad suggests that it has inadvertently brought land for development of housing though it is beset with many administrative problems. This, however, was also aided by the buoyant system of private developers in the city. On the other hand, Urban Land Ceiling has failed to enable the local authorities to acquire any land. This means that more innovative, fiscal measures to influence the market may be necessary in order to facilitate direct acquisition. However, such measures have to be based on a more sensitive understanding of the local land and housing markets.

The crucial question with respect to land is not really its availability but its adequate servicing. The local authorities, especially in the periphery, have failed to deliver in this respect. These problems can be overcome if the necessary financial assistance is forthcoming for these agencies. The second question concerns an adequate servicing of low-income settlements, especially with individual facilities. A recent report by AMC (1986) estimates that adequate servicing of 'slum' housing within the AMC limits will require only about 170 million rupees at 1984–85 prices. Even if we consider slum housing in metropolitan Ahmedabad, by 1991 the necessary investments may not exceed 420 million rupees. Compared to this, the public sector is likely to make an annual investment of almost 200 million rupees in public housing projects within the city. Thus only with a two year moratorium on housing construction by the public agencies, it would be possible to meet the needs of basic amenities in the slum areas.

A third issue related to land concerns the provision of legal tenure rights for land in existing slum settlements. It is extremely important to distinguish between tenure security (which implies the perception of a household's ability to continue to reside in a place without undue threats of eviction) and the legal freehold/leasehold ownership. Our findings indicate that though the security of tenure is important as a prerequisite for the upgradation process, the preference for legality is evident only at later stages in the life cycle and with higher income attainment. The current emphasis on legal tenure in the upgradation projects thus appears to be a value bias and is as misplaced as the emphasis on *pucca* shelter twenty years ago. It may lead to a host of unintended effects like high turnover, increase in prices and rents which will ultimately oust the lower income strata pushing them further into the tightening informal market and other over-crowded squatter settlements. The response, however, should be more positive if the demands have come from the local mass-based people's organisations which would mitigate the likely unintended effects.

DEMAND FOR HOUSING FINANCE

Most general reviews of housing finance systems in developing countries have indicated that at present only 10 to 15 per cent of the demand for housing finance is met through formal institutions (Renaud, 1984). In Ahmedabad, the formal institutional housing finance, mainly from the Apex Cooperative Society and the Housing Development Finance Corporation, has been disbursed to a very small proportion of owners. In a situation of limited supplies, the higher income groups are bound to enjoy better access to housing finance.

On the whole, the recent trends with the proposed National Housing Bank and the concessions in personal income tax are indicative of the government's attitude towards facilitating increased investments in housing. However, most of these benefits are not likely to filter down to the low-income strata. Concerted efforts for making the necessary housing finance available to the lower income groups are necessary particularly as their level of demand is low and well within the reach of the existing financial institutions. Besides, one of the major problems with the financial system is a lack of adequate system of grass roots level intermediaries. Thus, it is extremely necessary to develop a wide network for access to institutional housing finance. In this light, it may be worthwhile to review the possibility of organisations which have a strong network of committed field staff and can link housing finance to other developmental programmes. It may be also possible and beneficial to involve the large number of mass-based people's organisations and genuine non-governmental agencies which are already involved in such activities.

An additional aspect concerning housing finance relates to the need for finance for housing upgradation. Our studies indicate that the upgradation process is extremely limited in Ahmedabad despite the fact that the rates of residential mobility are very low. One of the major constraints in the upgradation process is a total lack of access to housing finance for this purpose. Thus though a large proportion of households feel severely constrained, they are unable to improve their houses. There is an urgent need for public and private sector agencies to be involved in this activity.

HOUSING SUPPLY SYSTEMS

The present continued efforts of both formal and informal sectors account for an average annual increase of about 15,000 housing units in the city. A part of this increase is through a sub-division of housing stock and not through new housing units. It is thus unlikely that given the present system of production, the requisite supply of housing will be forthcoming. For the public sector, the undue insistence on packaged product has limited the magnitude of its contribution.

The public sector agencies to a large extent depend on external assistance from the Housing and Urban Development Corporation and other international financing institutions for their projects. Unless the flow of funds increases, the public sector will not be able to increase its supply. More importantly, there is no effective land management strategy to ensure supply of land at appropriate locations given the fact that these agencies should cater to the low income needs. A large proportion of recent projects by the public sector have been concentrated at particular locations, simply because land was easily available even though it is locationally quite unsuitable for low-income groups. More importantly, however, it is essential to take a critical review of the product mix supplied by the public sector as well as a drastic redefinition in the role of the state especially in view of the housing support policy framework which is accepted as essential in the draft National Housing Policy paper of the Ministry of Urban Development (1987).

The role of the state today is unfortunately limited to packaged public housing with a few symbolic sites and services projects. A revision in its product mix is necessary by according the larger priority to a large-scale and coordinated land development programme to ensure supply of serviced land to different segments of the market. It must take up service upgrading for all the existing settlements as an on-going process, at societally determined minimum standards regardless of affordability. It should also provide technical assistance to different supply and user groups especially in areas of residential layouts, upgradation of existing stock, and infrastructure networks, and evolve mechanisms for housing finance system to fully utilise the available potential demand in this sector.

The private sector in the city has evolved different mechanisms for gaining access to land. They are thus less constrained by land availability. Their major limitations are with respect to the availability of finance. During the sixties and seventies, a dominant role was played by the Gujarat Cooperative Housing Finance Corporation (GCHFC). However, GCHFC has in the recent years, been facing severe resource constraints. Flow of housing finance from other sources, especially Housing Development Finance Corporation has been growing, but its extent so far has been quite limited. The potential demand for housing exists only with appropriate finance. It is thus likely that all the demand of the upper income groups and a very large part of the middle-income group will be met through the private sector, if the state simply facilitates housing finance.

The informal sector has so far managed without any support from the state and at times despite hindrances from it. The only major state support for this sector has been in the form of provision of services at the community level to the existing slum settlements. In view of the meagre efforts of the public and formal private sector to reach the urban poor, it is likely that the informal-squatters and quasi-legal housing will continue to be the dominant mode of absorption of the housing needs of the poor. In Ahmedabad, based on the income distribution and past trends, it is likely that the stock of informal housing may increase from its 1981 level of 118,000 units to about 280,000 units in 2001. Given this, the state would probably do well to ensure adequate infrastructural standards and provide technical and financial assistance for housing upgradation processes. In the new settlements, technical assistance for more suitable residential layouts may also be useful.

STRENGTHENING OF THE RENTAL MARKET

Although the preference for ownership is high for all groups, there is also a need for rental housing especially at early stages in the life cycle. However, in the light of the perceived threat of Rent Control Legislation and the bias of the local property tax assessment procedure towards owners*, nearly all the new housing built in the city is likely to be in the ownership market. On the other hand, there are high vacancy rates despite low levels of residential mobility. Further intra-urban mobility of households to improve their housing situation is generally inhibited in case of these households which enjoy low rents due to the protection from the Rent Control Legislation.

* The local property tax assessment for owned occupied premises is nearly one-tenth of that for a similar rental premise.

Analysts all over the world have in general, advocated moderate to drastic changes in the Rent Control (Malpezzi, 1984; Planning Commission, 1984; National Commission on Urbanisation, 1987). If the proposed amendments are likely to be implemented in the city, the following can be anticipated.

1. A reduction in the vacancy rate from its present level of 9.92 in the next decade. This would imply a decrease in housing requirements and correspondingly a decrease in investment and land requirements.

2. It is also likely that the rental market will be rejuvenated through efficient utilisation of unused floor space indices. At present in western AMC, the FSI utilisation is only 40 per cent of the permissible limits. Home owners are likely to build rental-housing at relatively lesser unit costs and thus lead to a decrease in effective demand for housing finance as well as land.

3. Though initially, this rental market is likely to cater to only the higher income households, increased mobility and filtering in the short run are likely to facilitate housing adjustment processes and in the long run generate a rental market for the low-income households in the formal sector as well.

FUTURE DIRECTIONS

Before concluding it is important to highlight two important directions for further efforts in this sector. At the local level, there is an urgent need to evolve an appropriate institutional mechanism to coordinate the activities of diverse agencies which influence the housing demand, supplies and the market itself. This institutional mechanism must also be within the perspective of a housing support policy framework.

No matter how effective such policy changes prove to be, the resource constraints identified earlier, clearly indicate continuing conflicts for distribution of such scarce resources. This suggests that even the most efficient and equitable policies will never be adequate enough. The housing question will, for a long time to come, essentially be in the realm of political struggles. This implies that it is very important to strengthen the organisational capacities of the more disadvantaged sections. This then, becomes an essential element of the overall housing strategy. It is the combined directions evolving from a totally redefined housing support policy framework with the grass roots strengthening of mass-based people's organisations which will take a quantum leap for the housing sector in the coming years.

Appendix

AHMEDABAD HOUSING SURVEY

As the primary survey formed the main basis for a large part of the analysis in the study, it was essential to design the survey carefully and in a statistically appropriate manner. Basically, the household is taken as the sampling unit in order to fulfill the study objectives. The Census of India's definition of household was adopted for this purpose.

SAMPLING FRAME

The sample design has to largely depend on the available sampling frame which should be a complete and up-to-date list of sample units. For our study, three sampling frames were considered, namely, the ration card registers, electoral rolls and the census enumerators' lists. The first one was rejected on the grounds of possible omissions, duplications and a total lack of conformity with the spatial sub-units for which certain basic statistics were available. The electoral rolls were quite recent and did not suffer from a large-scale under or over enumeration problems. However, these did not bear any relationship with the spatial units. Further, these would have been difficult to trace in field as there were no maps to accompany the lists at all.

The census enumeration lists, though a little outdated were found to be reliable and did not suffer from omissions or duplications. Furthermore, the samples were arranged in a hierarchical order of city/village, wards, enumeration blocks and dwellings. Thus, the spatial delineation was very clear and sketch maps were available for these spatial units up to dwelling levels for each block. This made the selection and identification of sample units easier and systematic. It was with these advantages in mind that we selected the census enumeration lists as the sampling frame for the study.

SAMPLE SIZE

The reliability of the estimates in the study depends to a great extent on the sample size and design. In order to determine the sample size with a desired level of confidence, it is necessary to have the frequency distribution for some of the important variables like housing value, price, housing tenure etc. However, the only information which was readily available pertained to the annual rental value for the area within the Municipal Corporation boundaries. With all its limitations, this can be considered as a proxy for distribution of dwellings by value. The distribution for 1980–81 gave the mean rental value at Rs. 385.43 with a standard deviation of Rs. 581.95. Thus the coefficient of variation was 151. Using the formula, suggested by Murthy (1967), the estimated sample size at 95 per cent level of confidence came to about 910 households.*

SAMPLING DESIGN

Selection of sample units was done in two stages. The first stage of selection pertained to census blocks. There were 4704 census enumeration blocks in the Ahmedabad Municipal Corporation area, and 1024 census blocks in the peripheral areas. From this total of 5728 blocks, it was decided to select 100 blocks in the first stage. Sample blocks were arranged randomly and through PPS (Probability Proportional to Size), 100 census blocks were selected.†
The selected blocks were plotted on the map to check the spatial distribution.

In the second stage of sample selection, ten per cent of the total households within each block were selected through a systematic

---

* The formula used was:

$$n = \frac{NC^2}{(N-1)\ e^2 + C^2}$$

Where: n = total sample size
N = total houses in the universe
C = coefficient of variation
e = level of significance

† The PPS method of selection has an advantage over simple random sampling for studies of this nature, as it provides for greater probability of selection for blocks which are well developed.

random sampling. Since each block, on an average had 90 to 100 households, it was decided that in order to get the requisite sample of 910, a uniform selection rate of 10 per cent from each block would be adequate. This also ensured that for the city level estimation, all the blocks will have equal weightage.

HOUSEHOLD SCHEDULES

The survey was based on the structured household schedules. For the actual field work, the schedules were translated in Gujarati, which is the local language. This was essential for the correct interpretation of terms during the survey. Detailed instructions were also given to the investigators on the basis of the pilot surveys. The major areas under which the information was collected are as follows:

A *Household Background*
   a. Details of age, sex, education, current activity etc., for each member in the household.
   b. Details of work, income and experience for each worker and other sources of income.
   c. Migration details for the head of household.
   d. Demographic changes in the household.
   e. Asset base inclusive of vehicles.

B *Current House*
   a. Details of location, age, duration of residence, tenure, size, etc.
   b. Details of current and initial situation, nature of changes made, satisfaction level, etc., for each attribute of size, materials and utilities.
   c. Activity patterns and satisfaction for use of facilities.
   d. Perception of best and worst aspect of current house.

C *Potential Mobility*
   a. Nature of consideration of potential mobility and reasons.
   b. Search process, type of house looking for, awareness and perception of market and details of houses seen.

D *Tenure and Expenditure Patterns*
   a. Total household expenditure on different major heads, debts.

    b. For renters—details of tenure, rents, other housing expenditure, renter-landlord relationship, awareness.

    c. For owners—mode of acquisition, process of building, housing finance, renting.

    d. Perception of market prices and rents.

    e. Details of other property, if any.

E *Past Residential Mobility*

    a. Basic details for all the previous houses since household formation.

    b. Search process for those who have moved in the last five years.

References

Abu-Lughod, J., and **Foley, M.M.** (1960), 'The Consumer Votes by Moving' in Foote, N.N., et al. (eds.), *Housing Choices and Housing Constraints*, New York.

Ahmedabad Municipal Corporation (AMC) (1985), *Project Proposal for Slum Upgradation for the City of Ahmedabad*, Vikas Centre for Development (mimeo).

Ahmedabad Municipal Corporation (AMC) (1976), *Report on Census of Slums in Ahmedabad*, Ahmedabad.

Ahmedabad Municipal Corporation (AMC) (1975), *Draft Revised Development Plan, 1975–85* (mimeo), Ahmedabad.

Ahmedabad Urban Development Authority (1986), *Annual Report, 1985–86* (mimeo), Ahmedabad.

Ahmedabad Urban Development Authority (n.d.), *Urban Housing Strategy* (mimeo), Ahmedabad.

Alonso, W. (1964), *Location and Land Use*, Cambridge, Massachusetts.

Baross, P., and **Martinez, E.** (1977), 'Upgrading Low-income Residential Areas in Developing Countries: The Social Organization of Decision-making', in Angal, S., et al. (eds.), *Low-income Housing: Technology and Policy*, Bangkok.

Bhatt, M., and **Chavda, V.** (1979), *Anatomy of Urban Poverty*, Ahmedabad.

Bhatt, M., and **Chavda, V.** (n.d.), *Some Aspects of Cooperative Housing Societies in Ahmedabad City*, Ahmedabad.

Boni, M. (1985), 'Evaluation of Slum Improvement Programme: A Case Study of Ahmedabad', Unpublished dissertation, School of Planning, Ahmedabad.

Brown, L.A., and **Moore, E.G.** (1970), 'Intra-urban Migration Process: A Perspective' in Bourne L.S. (ed.), *Internal Structure of the City*, London.

Chaudhari, Mitali (1984), 'Policy Implications of Housing Needs: A Case Study of Ahmedabad', Unpublished dissertation, School of Planning, Ahmedabad.

Conway, D. (1982), 'Self-help Housing, the Commodity Nature of Housing Deficit: Continuing the Turner-Burgees Debate', *Antipode*, Vol. 14, No. 2, pp. 40–45.

Datta, S.S. (n.d.), *Land Policies in Human Settlements: A Review of Current Practise in India*, TCPO, New Delhi (mimeo).

Desai, P., and **Srimali, S.** (1984), *Environmental Improvement Programme of AMC*, School of Planning, Ahmedabad (mimeo).

Deo, V. (1982), 'Evaluation of Urban Land Ceiling Act', Unpublished dissertation, School of Planning, Ahmedabad.

Deshpande, S. (1976), 'Resettling a Squatter Resettlement: Janata Colony', in *Economic and Political Weekly*, 11 and 17 April.

D'Souza, J.B. (n.d.), *Housing for the Forgotten Man*, Housing and Urban Development Corporation (HUDCO), New Delhi.

Edwards, M. (1983), 'Residential Mobility in a Changing Housing Market, the Case of Bucaramuanga, Colombia', in *Urban Studies*, 20, pp. 131–45

Engineer, Asghar Ali (1985), 'Ahmedabad: From Caste to Communal Violence', in *Economic and Political Weekly*, Vol. XX, No. 15, April 13, pp. 628–30.

Follain, J., and **Jimminez, E.** (1983), 'The Demand for Housing Characteristics in Developing Countries: Colombia, Korea and the Philippines', Metropolitan Studies Programme, Occasional Paper, Syracuse University.

Geertz, C. (1963), *Peddlers and Princes: Social Change and Economic Modernization in Two Indonesian Towns*, Chicago.

Gilbert, A., and **Gugler, J.** (1982), *Cities, Poverty and Development*, London.

Gillion, K.L. (1968), *Ahmedabad: A Study in Indian Urban History*, Berkeley.

Goodman, J.L. (1976), 'Housing Consumption Disequilibrium and Local Residential Mobility' in *Environment and Planning*, Vol. 8, pp. 855–74.

Gujarat Slum Clearance Board (1983), *Slums in Ahmedabad*, Core Consultant, Ahmedabad.

Gupta, D.B. (1985), *Urban Housing in India*, World Bank Staff Working Paper, No. 730, Washington D.C.

Government of India (1964), *Report of the Committee on Urban Land Policy*, New Delhi.

Ingram, G. (1981), *Housing Demand in the Developing Metropolis—Estimates from Bogota, and Cali, Colombia*, Staff Working Paper No. 663 (1984), Urban and Regional Economics Division, The World Bank, Washington D.C.

Isaac, M. (n.d.), *Management of Public Housing: A Study of the Working of the Gujarat Housing Board*, Indian Institute of Management, Ahmedabad (mimeo).

Jimminez, Emmanuel (1982), 'The Extent of Housing Improvement in a Squatter Upgrading Project', in *Nagarlok*, April-June, No. 2, pp. 39–53.

Johnstone, M. (1985), 'Urban Housing and Housing Policy in Peninsular Malaysia', *International Journal of Urban and Regional Research*, Vol. 8, No. 4, pp. 497–529.

Jones, C. (1979), 'Housing: The Element of Choice', in *Urban Studies*, Vol. 16, pp. 197–204.

Joshi, H., and **Joshi, V.** (1976), *Surplus Labour and the City: A Study of Bombay*, New Delhi.

Kashyap, S.P., et al. (1984), *Facets of Urban Economy*, TCPO New Delhi.

Kalyani, K. (1986), 'Slum Upgradation Process: A Case Study of Madras', Unpublished dissertation, School of Planning, Ahmedabad.

King, A.T., and **Mieszkowski, Peter** (1973), 'Racial Discrimination, Segregation, and the Relative Price of Housing', in *Journal of Political Economy*, 81, May, pp. 590–606.

Kothari, Sujata (1988), 'Decision Making Process in Policy Formulation and Implementation', Unpublished dissertation, School of Planning, Ahmedabad.

Lancaster, K.J. (1966), 'A New Approach to Consumer Theory', in *Journal of Political Economy*, 74, pp. 132–57.

Lewis, W.A. (1958), 'Economic Development with Unlimited Supplies of Labour', in Agarwala, H.N., and S.P. Singh (eds.), *The Economics of Underdevelopment*, New Delhi.

Malpezzi et al. (1985), *Housing Demand in Developing Countries*, World Bank Staff Working Paper No. 733, World Bank, Washington D.C.

Mathur, O.P. (1986), 'Growing Urban Housing Needs', paper presented at workshop on *Housing in Urban Development*, ICSSR, New Delhi.

Mayo, K. (1978), 'Theory and Estimation in the Economics of Housing Demand', Paper presented at the meeting of the American Economic Association, Chicago, mimeo.

Mayo, Stephen (1983), *Housing Demand in Developing Countries*, Urban Development Department, World Bank, Washington D.C.

Mehta, Barjor (1980), 'Urban Housing—Objective Realities for the Poor', Unpublished dissertation, School of Architecture, Ahmedabad.

Mehta, Meera (1982), 'Urban Labour in the Lower Strata: A Case Study of Slums in Ahmedabad', Unpublished dissertation, Gujarat University, Ahmedabad.

Mehta, Meera (1982a), 'Urban Housing Processes and the Poor: A Case Study of Ahmedabad', in *Nagarlok*, April-June, pp. 106–29.

Mehta, Meera, and **Mehta, Dinesh** (1987), *Evolution of Low-Income Settlements*, Part of the HSMI Research Cycle (mimeo).

Mehta, M., Mehta, D., and **Swamy H.M.** (1986), 'Residential Land Management in the Fringe Area of Ahmedabad: Towards a Policy Perspective', paper presented at the workshop on *Urban Land Management* at School of Planning, Ahmedabad.

Menon, Vasanthi (1985), 'A Review of Modern Spatial Planning Principles', Unpublished dissertation, School of Planning, Ahmedabad.

Ministry of Urban Development, Govt. of India (1987), *Draft National Housing Policy*, New Delhi (mimeo).

Mitra, A., et al. (1980), *Indian Cities: Their Industrial Structure, Inmigration and Capital Investment, 1961–71*, New Delhi.

Mohan, R., and **Villamizar, R.** (1980), *The Evolution of Land Values in the Context of Rapid Urban Growth: A Case Study of Bogota and Cali*, Urban and Regional Report, No. 80–10, World Bank, Washington D.C.

Mukherjee, S.R., and **Bannerjee, S.K.** (1978), 'Some Aspects of Internal Annual Migration in India', *Sarvekshana*, New Delhi.

Murthy, M.N. (1967), *Sampling Theory and Methods*, Calcutta.

Nath, Narendra C. (1976), 'Housing the Urban Poor—A Critique', unpublished dissertation, School of Planning, Ahmedabad.

National Building Organisation (NBO) (1984), *Handbook of Housing Statistics in India: 1978–79, 1982–83*, New Delhi.

National Commission on Urbanisation, Ministry of Urban Development (1987), *First Interim Report*, New Delhi.

Planning Commission (1983), *Shelter for the Urban Poor and Slum Improvement*, Report of the Task Force on Housing and Urban Development, IV, New Delhi.

Planning Commission (1952), *First Five Year Plan*, New Delhi.

Papola, T.S. (1978), *Informal Sector in an Urban Economy: A Study of Ahmedabad*, Lucknow (mimeo).

Paul, S. (1972), 'Housing: A Case of Subsidising the Rich', *Economic and Political Weekly*, May.

Polinsky, A.M., and **Elwood** (1979), 'An Empirical Reconciliation of Micro and Grouped Estimates of the Demand for Housing', *Review of Economics*, March, 1979, Vol. 2, No. 1, pp. 199–205.

Quigley, J.M., and **Weinberg, D.H.** (1977), 'Intra-Urban Residential Mobility', in *International Regional Science Review*, Vol. 2, No. 1, pp. 41–66.

Quigley, J. (1979), 'What Have we Learnt about Urban Housing Markets?', in Miseszkowski and Straszheim (eds.), *Current Issues in Urban Economics*, Baltimore.

Rangan, H. (1983), 'Residential Choice Behaviour of Low-Income Households', Unpublished dissertation, School of Planning, Ahmedabad.

Reddy, S.S. (1984), 'Computer Based Analysis for Affordable Shelter', Unpublished dissertation, School of Planning, Ahmedabad.

Renaud, B. (1984), *Housing and Financial Institutions in Developing Countries: An Overview*, World Bank Staff Working Paper, No. 658, Washington D.C.

Rosen, S. (1974), 'Hedonic Prices and Implicit Markets: Product Differentiation in Pure Competition', *Journal of Political Economy*, pp. 34–55.

Rossi, P. (1955), *Why Families Move*, Glencoe.

Santos, M. (1979), *The Shared Space, The Two Circuits of the Urban Economy in Underdeveloped Countries*, London.

Seek, N.H. (1983), 'Adjusting Housing Consumption: Improve or Move', *Urban Studies*, No. 20, pp. 455–69.

Sen, Kaushik (1988), 'A Study of Displaced Textile Workers in Ahmedabad', Unpublished dissertation, School of Planning, Ahmedabad.

Sharma, Utpal (1983), 'Housing Preferences and Incremental Housing Construction', Unpublished dissertation, School of Planning, Ahmedabad.

Sinha, Alpana (1982), 'Density, Design and Cost Study at Residential Level', Unpublished dissertation, School of Planning, Ahmedabad.

Sompura, C. (1983), 'Residential Structure and Its Evolution: A Historical Analysis of Ahmedabad City', Unpublished dissertation, School of Planning, Ahmedabad.

Strassman, W.P. (1975), 'Industrialized Systems Building for Developing Countries: A Discouraging Prognosis', as quoted in Nath (1976).

Strassman, W.P. (1982), *Transformation of Urban Housing*, World Bank, Washington D.C.

Straszheim, Mahlon, R. (1973), 'Estimation of the Demand for Urban Housing Services from Household Interview Data', in *The Review of Economics and Statistics*, Vol. V, No. 1, February.

Stegman, M.A. (1969), 'Accessibility Models and Residential Location', in *JAIP*, Jan., Vol. 35, No. 1, pp. 22–29.

Struyk, R. (1982), 'Upgrading Existing Dwellings: An Element in the Housing Strategies of Developing Countries', in *The Journal of Developing Areas*, 17, October, pp. 67–76.

Swamy, H.M.S. (1983), 'Labour Absorption and Earnings: A Case Study of Lower Strata Workers in Bangalore', Unpublished dissertation, School of Planning, Ahmedabad.

Trivedi, P. (1985), 'Impact of ULCRA on Housing Industry' (mimeo), School of Planning, Ahmedabad.

Turner, John (1972), *Housing by People*, London.

Vastu-Shilpa Foundation for Studies and Research in Environmental Design (VSF) (1984), *East Ahmedabad Development Plan, Towards a Conceptual Strategy*, Ahmedabad.

Wadhwa, K. (1983), 'A Evaluation of Urban Land Ceiling Legislation—A Case Study of Ahmedabad', *Nagarlok*, Vol. 15, No. 2, pp. 76–86.

Wadhwa, K. (1987), *Role of Private Sector in Urban Housing—Case Study of Ahmedabad*, New Delhi.

World Bank (1975), *Housing: Sector Policy Paper*, Washington D.C.